Introduction
Black Panther Inspiration For Prisoners?

While every precaution has been taken in the preparation of this book, the publisher assumes no responsibility for errors or omissions, or for damages resulting from the use of the information contained herein.

BLACK PANTHER INSPIRATION

First edition. May 14, 2018.

Written by Black Panthers.

Bread of Life

Because he hath set his love upon me, therefore will I deliver him:
I will set him on high, because he hath known my name.
Psalms 91:14
(KJV)

Black Panther Inspiration; Giving Our Hearts to God

What's up readers? My name is Antonio, but most people call me *Buck. The book that you are reading is about how I and many others have chased after their own desires.*

We have all put many things before God and His son Jesus, and Their will for our lives. We have been selfish- putting our own needs and satisfaction before God's. By placing and putting *things before God, we have committed sin against Him. We have also sinned by loving materialistic things and others more than we loved Him. But God is the only reason that we are blessed with anything that is good in the first place.*

God has loved us from the very first moment that he created us. God knows all of our hearts and wants us to give them to him willingly. God has always and will always love us all the same. We are all created n His image and possess many of His traits. Just like God, we want people to love us willingly, without having to force ourselves upon them. God has given us love that is unmatchable.

Many people have thought and said that they loved us, but have shown flaws in their love because they can't help who they are- *human. All it takes is for us to make one mistake and some people will take their affection and love away from us without any* remorse. But that is not God's way.

He has sacrificed his only son so that those who believe in Him should not die, but have eternal life (John 3:16). God sacrificed the life of His only son, Jesus Christ, for us. We were sinners but yet he still made a way for us to live forever. No one has ever shown us this kind of love.

Consider this:

Imagine that a man breaks into your home while you and our family sleep, forces himself on one of your daughters and kills her. Could you forgive the man? Most would answer "NO!"

Now, let's take it a step deeper:

The offender is taken to trial and given the death penalty. During sentencing, the judge tells you that he would be willing to allow the man to live but only if you will sacrifice the life of your only living daughter. To our human minds this seems like a ludicrous suggestion that no one would even entertain.

This scenario is exactly what God did for us. Some of us have raped, stolen, and killed. We have all sinned against God and against others and all sin is the same in the eyes of God. Even though we have all sinned against Him, because God loved us so much, He sent and sacrificed his only son so that we could have another chance at life. Now that's love!

I don't know about you but no one has ever come close to loving me *that much. We all want to be loved and so does God All God wants from us in return is our hearts, our obedience, and our love. He wants us to accept Jesus as our Christ and savior. He wants us to ask for forgiveness and repent from our sin.*

I have decided to accept Christ and I hope you will do the same. This book is dedicated to God! I appreciate all that He has done for me and my heart belongs to Him!

As you read this book, I hope you will find help in difficult situations and learn to always love the Lord God with all of your heart, soul, and might. I hope you will love Him in everything that you do, remembering that He loved us first. I hope that you enjoy yourself as you walk with me. Thanks for reading and God Bless you!!!

Loving God in Everything We Do

God loves all who love Him and our love is all that He desires. He will test us to see if we are sincere and put our heart through the fire.

We were created by Him and are His prized possessions. Therefore, we should willingly give our lives to Him and bring our flesh under subjection.

He loved us first to show us how t should be done. So follow the leader and give Him back the same in return.

If a drum is for the ear and a mouth is for the tongue, then cherish God by giving Him the love from our hearts in everything that we do.

Poem by Antonio E. Walker

Way of Life

You must love the Lord God with all your heart, all your soul, and your entire mind. This is the first and greatest commandment.
Matthew 22:37-38
(NLT)

<u>*INTRODUCTION PRAYER*</u>

Psalm 86:

A prayer of David;

1 Hear me, Lord, and answer me, for I am poor and needy.

2 Guard my life, for I am faithful to you; save your servant who trusts in you.

You are my God; 3 have mercy on me, Lord, for I call to you all day long. 4 Bring joy to your servant, Lord, for I put my trust in you. 5 You, Lord, are forgiving and good, abounding in love to all who call to you.

6 Hear my prayer, Lord; listen to my cry for mercy. 7 When I am in distress, I call to you, because you answer me.

8 Among the gods there is none like you, Lord; no deeds can compare with yours. 9 All the nations you have made

will come and worship before you, Lord; they will bring glory to your name. 10 For you are great and do marvelous deeds; you alone are God. 11 *Teach me your way, Lord, that I may rely on your faithfulness; give me an undivided heart, that I may fear your name.*

12 *I will praise you, Lord my God, with all my heart;*

I will glorify your name forever. 13 *For great is your love toward me; you have delivered me from the depths, from the realm of the dead.*

14 *Arrogant foes are attacking me, O God; ruthless people are trying to kill me—they have no regard for you.*

15 *But you, Lord, are a compassionate and gracious God,*

slow to anger, abounding in love and faithfulness.

16 *Turn to me and have mercy on me; show your strength in behalf of your servant; save me, because I serve you just as my mother did.* 17 *Give me a sign of your goodness, that my enemies may see it and be put to shame,*

for you, Lord, have helped me and com-forted me.

Chapter One

Believing

In

Something Better

Jesus said unto him, If thou canst believe, all things are possible to him that believeth.

Mark 9:23 (KJV)

Bread of Life

I am come a light into the world, that whosoever believeth on me should not abide in darkness.
John 12:46
(KJV)

Believing in Something Better

I have been out of foster care for fifteen years now, and from the first day that I ran away to this moment, I have been locked up inside of a jail or prison cell for around a total of 104 months. That is exactly eight years and eight months out of fifteen years. When I first add up this total, I am shocked to realize that I have spent over half of the last fifteen years of my life locked up.

That is what makes me want to leave selling drugs alone. I look back on my life and see that I am not a good drug dealer. I made plenty of money, had lots of beautiful women, and loved all of the attention and respect I received when I was selling drugs. Even so, now I am alone with nothing.

The only one that has been there for me unconditionally is God, Jesus, and the Holy Spirit. I was incarcerated at one of the worst prisons in the state of Georgia. All around me, guys were killing, robbing, raping, and committing other malicious acts to one another.

I used to ask God why He allowed e to go to a close security prison around all of these types of people. He quickly answered telling me that I had been running the streets, selling drugs, and hanging out with the exact same kind of people, so there was no use in whining about it now. I thought about this answer and realized that (As Always!) He was right. From that day forth, I accepted His decision and just prayed that He would protect me and keep me out of harm's way.

*I served twenty-six months at Smith State Prison and learned a lot of life-changing things. The most important of which was that I did not have to believe everything that the devil and everyone else were telling me because they told many lies. I learned that I wasn't ug*ly, but I was a beautiful creation of God. I used to *think that the on-*

ly thing I was good at was cooking cocaine, but was during that time that God revealed to me talents and gifts that I never knew I had. He also showed me that everyone in the world endures trials and tribulations, not just me. Trials are given and used to strengthen and prepare us for the coming journey that Jesus is going to take us on in life.

I do not know who my biological father is, but I have found my real father. He is the father of the fatherless. I have been listening to people all of my life and wasting y time trying to please them, when all along I have had a loving friend in Christ Jesus who sees me and loves me for being me. I love God, Jesus, and the Holy Spirit because they have never lied or tried to let bring me down; but instead have given me a future filled with blessings in return for my love. If I will believe in God, I won't *have to sell drugs or hurt people to make money. I can trust Him to provide for me and make me prosperous. I can have whatever I desire as long as I am obedient and do his will. I believe that Jesus Christ is my Lord and Savior. I believe I can do all things through him because he promises to strengthen me. I believe that I do not have to live n darkness or go to hell because my sins have been forgiven. I believe that I have been saved and made into a new creature. All these things God has promised me and I know that He is a God that does not lie.*

I do not believe that I have to continue to live a wicked life. All that I believe is what God tells me. I now believe that my life is going to change and that change will be for the better.

Believing in Something Better

I may not be a lion or king of the jungle, but I do believe that I can roar.

I know that I cannot fly, but with faith I do believe that I can soar.

I do believe in a Devine purpose that is greater than you and me. I have belief in a God so powerful that he allowed Moses to part the sea.

I believe that Jesus Christ sacrificed His life for the world. I don't believe in eating clams, but I do believe that they make beautiful pearls.

I love the sunshine, but also believe in stormy weather. I know that right now I am locked up in prison, but when I look at my future, I do believe in something better.

Poem by Antonio E Walker

Way of Life

IF YOU CONFESS WITH your mouth that Jesus is Lord and believe in your heart that God raised Him from the dead, you will be saved.

For it s believing in our heart that you are made right with God, and it is by confessing with your mouth that you are saved.

Romans 10:9-10
(NLT)

PRAYER;

YAHAWAH My Heavenly Father, may I love You in all things and above all things.

May I reach the joy which You have prepared for me in Heaven. Nothing is good that is against Your Will, and all that is good comes from Your Hand. Place in my heart a desire to please You and fill my mind with thoughts of Your Love,

so that I may grow in Your Wisdom and enjoy Your Peace.
AMEN!!!

Chapter Two
False
Beliefs

Only simpletons believe everything they are told.
Proverbs 14:15
(NLT)

Bread of Life

AND FOR THIS CAUSE God shall send them strong delusion, that they shall believe a lie: That they all might be damned who believed not the truth, but had pleasure in unrighteousness.
2 Thessalonians 2:11-12
(KJV)

Listening to Lies

One of the worst things that a person can let into their life is a negative person. Life is already hard enough, then we allow others to bring us down. This has been a problem for me all my life. I have tried to impress or be accepted by others since I was a young child. The harder I tried, the more I became a different person. I would do and say things that I thought made me look cool. The problem with doing that is that it so hard to continue to be someone you really aren't. *After a while, I came to realize that some people are going to down you anyway. No matter what I did or who I was, people were going to talk about me both positively and negatively.*

Trying to not listen to the negative things that people say is not easy at all, especially for me. I have been talked about my whole life. I have heard so many negative things that you would think that I would be used to it by now, but that is the farthest thing from the truth. Because I am a really sensitive person, my feelings have been hurt constantly. Sometimes my feelings were hurt so bad that I would shed a few tears.

One of the things that hurt me the most was when people talked about my teeth. I have heard people say some very creative things about my buck teeth and have been called all kinds of names such as "Bucky", "walrus", "beaver", and many more. My peers gave me the nickname "Buck". After hearing people call me so *many degrading names I ended up accepting Buck because it* didn't sound as bad to me.

As you can probably guess, I have very low self-esteem and always get shy around other people. I feel that, by being myself, I could never please others and whatever perception they had of me, I accepted as the truth. I could be feeling like I was handsome man and a really attractive person; then, out of nowhere, someone would call me ugly and instantly that's exactly how I felt multiplied by ten. I wouldn't just feel unattractive, *but like I was the ugliest creature God ever created. I would ask God why I was not handsome or fine to the ladies like other guys I saw.*

All of my life I have hated cameras or having pictures taken of me. I never liked any picture that was taken of me.

I have always been a person who dreams and set goals at a very high level. I grew up thinking that I could have and accomplish whatever I wanted as long as I put my mind to it. That is why I have always been fairly successful in the things that I set my mind to do. When I would share my plans and goals with others who I thought were my friends, they would say something negative or downing.

Once, I met a really gorgeous lady and wanted to show her that I would make a good companion. I started out just being me. I bought her flowers, wrote poems for her, listened to her every word, and was an all-around gentleman toward her. Then I let a couple of guys who I thought knew more about women than me give me some bad advice. They told me that women hated a guy that was too nice and didn't want a man to give them too much *attention. Because they had a lot of women, I listened to them and changed how I treated and stopped being me.*

Before long, she was tired of the new me. She told me that she was looking for something different n a man, and she thought she had found that in me. She said she was glad that I had shown my true colors before she fell in love with me. She was open to remaining friends, but she would not date me anymore. After that conversation I felt like a fool. When I was being myself, she was really thinking about letting me be her man. Because I listened to other peoples' lies and opinions, I had just messed up the *opportunity to be with a really gorgeous woman. And, BOY, was she FINE!*

Believing Others

DO NOT LISTEN TO THE beliefs and opinions about us that people will always make 3e

Because if we are in need of help or guidance we should get on our knees and ask God to show us the next step we need to take.

We will constantly be slandered or ridiculed with hostility and hate,

But we have to be patient and endure because the devil is going to continue to test our faith.

Honor and obey the truth that is found only in God's word

And quit being deceived by the words that are said and everything that is heard.

Every second we must strive to get away from deception and to move away from negativity a little further.

So keep your mind and thoughts positive and stop believing in the tales and fabrications of others.

Poem by Antonio E. Walker

Way of Life

The seeds that fell on the footpath represent those who hear the message, only to have the devil come and take it away from their hearts and prevent them from believing and being saved.

Luke 8:12

(NLT)

Prayer

Heavenly Father,
I come to you on this day asking for your help. I have been believing in the lies that others and satan have been putting into my mind. I have found the truth that is in your word Lord, and I
know that I can have all the promises that are in there as long as
I have faith in you and believe that your son Jesus Christ died for my sins and confess with my mouth that He is my savior. I
believe in your pan for my life and I accept it as my own.
Amen!

Chapter Three

Robbing Our Father

*Will a man rob God? Yet ye have robbed me. But ye say,
wherin have we robbed thee? In tithes and in offerings.*

Malachi 3:8
(KJV)

Robbing God

Shamed to say, I have stolen from God. Going to church as a child, I would steal from the collection plate. When all of the kids would be let out to go home, I would sneak back into the room and take the money. I'd go home and spend the money at the store up the street. *I have always had a problem with taking things that I wanted.*

I had behavior problems in school. I had an issue with being told what to do. The teachers sent home notes or came to my house and speak to my mother. I would get a whooping and be cussed out. I would return to school and behave for a few days. Then I would be back to my old ways. To try to control me, the teacher would move my desk to the front of the room beside hers. If she left candy, peanuts, or other things on her desk, I would take them at recess or lunch time. One time, the teacher left the money she had collected for school pic-tures laying on her desk. I took about five envelopes. She did not no-tice that that the envelopes were gone until the pictures came back and the parents of the kids' whose money I'd taken complained.

I was very good at stealing. The only time I got caught was when I was six. I went into a store that sold candy bars. I saw an Almond Joy candy bar that said free movie ticket on the wrapper. I thought that there was a movie ticket inside. I looked around and, when I thought no one was looking, put the candy bar into my pocket and walked out of the store. I had only taken a couple of steps when a man told me to come with him. I don't know why I didn't run, but I went to him. He took me by the *arm and led me back into the store. He called the police. When the police saw my young age, they looked at the man like he was crazy. One of the officers, a woman, offered to pay the price of the candy bar.*

The man refused and insisted on pressing charges against me. The officers filed the report and took me home to my mother. They ex-

*plained to her that I would have to go before a juvenile court judge.
When the left, I wished I could have gone with them because my mom
give me one of the best beatings that I ever received.*

*In court, the judge gave me a warning. He told me that if I ever
stole anything else. He would lock me up with the bad guys. I
promised him that I would not steal anymore; but that did not stop
me from stealing, it just made me more cautious. From that day
forth, when I stole something, I made sure that there was no way that
it could be tracked back to me and I never got caught again; until I
read Malachi 3:8.*

*The Lord has caught not only me, but everyone in this world that
does not give Him tithes and offerings. Everything we make is to be
divided with God. We are to give ten percent of our earnings. We are
to pay our dues to the churches which are His storehouses and temples. We need not worry about what is done with the money or if t is
used properly. The Lord will handle and take care of any false deeds.
We should pray and ask God to lead us in delivering the tithes to His
desired location. All that is asked of us is to be obedient. He knows
everything and will bless al cheerful givers with more than they can
use. He tells us in his word to test and try Him.*

*I do not want to steal or rob from anyone anymore, and certainly
not from my God who has made it possible for me to have n the* first
place. Let's quit robbing God. Let's make sure that His *storehouses
have plenty of meat and food for His temples by paying our tithes and
offerings.*

Paying Our Dues

The Lord sometimes gives and He also takes away.

He created everything that is in the heavens and earth, so it is His to use anyway.

If we have obtained wealth then we should also be willing to share. To keep anything that is His form Him, is something that we should not dare.

His tithes and offerings are wanted from every living and capable being.

If we are obedient to give them, He will bless us past our wildest dreams.

We should try and keep God happy by constantly paying our dues. But if you want to continue robbing Him, then it is your soul that you have to lose.

Poem by Antonio E. Walker

Way of Life

Bring all the tithes into the storehouse so there will be enough food in my temple. "If you do", says the Lord of Heaven's Armies, "I will open the windows of heaven for you. I will pour out blessing so great that you won't have enough room to take it in! Try It! Put Me to the test!"
Malachi 3:10
(NLT)

Prayer:

O loving and kind YAHAWAH, have mercy. Have pity upon me and take away the awful stain of my transgressions. Oh, wash me, cleanse me from this guilt. Let me be pure again. For I admit my shameful deed-it haunts me day and night. It is against you and you alone I sinned and did this terrible thing.

You saw it all, and your sentence against me is just. Create in me a new, clean heart, O YAHAWAH, filled with clean thoughts

and right desires. Don't toss me aside, banished forever from your presence. Don't take Your Holy Spirit from me. Restore to me again the joy of your salvation, and make me willing to obey you. Amen
(Psalm 51:1-12 TLB)

Chapter Four

Stolen
Identity

Do not steal. Do not deceive or cheat one another. Leviticus 19:11

(NLT)

Bread of Life

Whoso is partner with a thief hateth his own soul: he heareth cursingand bewrayeth it not.

Proverbs 29:24
(KJV)

Stealing Identities

I LIVED WITH A FRIEND for a couple weeks in Atlanta, Georgia. I was low on money at the time and didn't want to return to Columbus, my hometown, without any money. My friend told me he knew a woman who would help us make $500 to $1000 in a day. That sounded like music to my ears, so I told him to call her. We were instructed to meet her at a Chic-Fila restaurant.

She was waiting for us when we arrived. We got out of y friend's car and got into hers- a brand new *Yukon Denali.*

As we rode, the woman explained the details of making a lot of fast, easy money. The whole scheme involved check cashing. We would be given checks that varied in amount and would be given 40% of each check. We would first have to obtain fake IDs and social security numbers. We would also have to get passports and give them to her. She would do the rest. This seemed simple, so I agreed. I figured all that I would have to do was cash 10 checks for about $1000 a piece and I would have $400 to go back home with. Once we agreed, the woman took us to Walgreens where we got the passports. We gave her the passports and four small pictures of our faces. She took us back to Chic-Fila and dropped us off.

The next day, the woman called and instructed us to meet her at a Zaxby's. When we arrived, she gave each of us a social security card and a driver's license, both of which looked just like the real *ones. The names on the cards belonged to someone whose identity had been stolen. We had their social security number and birth date and were told to memorize their information. We were told to* forge the person's signature on the back of the cards. Then she *took us to another Yukon Denali and told us to get in. There were six other people in the truck, all of whom were trying to make some quick money just like us.*

We were all given five checks each. My checks were for $1300, $500, $700, $300, and $200. The sum of these was $3000. We were *taken to a number of grocery stores, liquor stores, check cashing places, and service stations. We put rubber cement on our fingers to hide our fingerprints. The checks were real and easy to cash. We had to take turns cashing the checks, with each person going in a different store. We began at 10:30 AM, and didn't get done until 8:00 PM. I was only able to cash four of the five checks id been given, but at the end of the day, I ended up with $920.*

I was extremely happy and decided to keep doing this until I had saved up enough money to buy a kilo of cocaine, which cost about $1800 at the time. I told myself that all I had to do was save $750 per day for a month. Then I would have enough money to buy a kilo and return to Columbus on top.

In no time, I had saved about $3300 and was doing well. I got high and partied with m friend some nights. We were supposed to be ready at 9:30 AM or we would miss the ride. On one particular morning, we woke up late and were not able to go.

We went home disappointed.

Later that day, someone told us that when one of the girls tried to cash a check, the store called the police. It seems that the checks were leaving a paper trail and the detectives had notified all of the local check cashing places. The girl told the police that there were other people in the Denali trying to cash checks also. The police arrested everyone. From that day on, I decided to never mess with cashing checks again and went back to Columbus.

A Thief in the Night

Thou shall not steal is a commandment that God enforces and demands.

So if you do it, do not be surprised if you lose your hands.

People work hard to get the things that their hearts want to obtain To out of nowhere come and take it, is something that we should be ashamed.

There are many who are lazy who don't want to work for the things *they like,*

But if they see another who has it, then they make plans to swipe.

Larceny is a sin and there is no way that we can say it is right, For if the sun has went down and we have stolen from someone. We are then a thief in the night.

Poem by Antonio E Walker

Way of Life

If you are a thief, quit stealing. Instead, use your hands for good hard
work, and then give generously to others in need.
Ephesians 4:28
(NLT)

Prayer

Lord,

Forgive me for stealing from others. I know that was very dishonest and I repent and promise not to do it again. I have also

stolen and robbed out of your desired tithes and offerings. I now know that everything is yours anyway and I appreciate you blessing me with the opportunity to give back to You.

Thank You, Amen!

Chapter Five

Me,

Myself, and

I

For if a man think himself to be something, when he is nothing, he deceiveth himself.

Galatians 6:3
(KJV)

Bread of Life

HE THAT IS OF A PROUD heart stirreth up strife: But he that putteth his trust n the Lord shall be made fat. He that trusteth n his own

heart is a fool: But whoso walketh wisely, he shall be delivered.

Proverbs 28:25-26 (KJV)

Persistent Love

One of the things that life n the drug game did to me was that it made me a loner. To this very day I trust a selective few individuals. When I jumped into the game, I was a very young man who was kind, helpful, and nice toward people. I learned the hard way, from experience, that I was destined from the beginning to fail. There is no place for nice guys while running in the streets. I was very kind to my customers. I was happy to do whatever they wanted, I did. As long as they spent their money with me, I felt that it was my duty to cater to them. A lot of drug dealers credit the users and, when they didn't have the money owed, they would beat them up. I, on the other hand, would not give the users anything on credit. I knew that the user would start dodging you if they owed large sums of money and start shopping with the next dealer. You would be lucky if you caught up with them at all. I would just give them $20 worth of crack and tell them they owed me nothing. This got me so many customers that I cannot remember or count them all.

The thing about the drug game s that it plays by its own rules. I was set up by the same customers that I dedicated myself to serving, while the dealers that beat them and talked to them like they were low-down, dirty dogs are still free. The users respect the violent dealers. They fear the violent dealers. When questioned by the police, who do you think the users set up? They pick "Mr. Niceguy"- Me.

When I first sat back and analyzed this, I became very angry. I was so nice to them and they repaid me by sending me to prison, not once, but twice. Now, I am not blaming anyone for being in prison. No, I take full responsibility for my actions. If I was that kind of person, I would have snitched on someone else to get out of jail or get a lesser sentence.

I could not see getting myself out of trouble by sending someone else to prison even though they may have been committing a crime. If

I was going to lock people up for doing wrong, I would have stayed n school and become a police officer or law enforcement officer.

I am a really emotional person and I guess I get a little depressed at how people will treat others, even those who go out of their way to please them. In saying that, I am not just talking about the street game, but the world in general. The more I went through in life to be nice to others, the more I was slapped n the face with ungratefulness.

As I got older, I started hating and resenting people. If a person made me mad in any kind of way, I went off on them and tried to hurt them. I adopted a new approach to handling all people. I was nice to everyone. They began with a clean slate; but if for any reason they crossed me or did something I felt was grimy or low-down, we instantly became enemies. The game and life made me cold-hearted.

It has taken a lot of time, faith, and prayed to overcome those feelings toward others. Without God, Jesus, and the Holy Spirit, it would be impossible. It takes God's power to cast out the *spirits that have possessed my mind, making me think that everyone is the same.*

The more I read my Bible, the more I learn to be patient toward others. The Word of God has shown me that I am exactly like the people that I resented for hurting me. I have hurt the only one in my life that has always loved me no matter what I did. Even though God has always treated me kindly and always loved me, I was ungrateful and disobedient and continued to sin. I have treated God very unfairly.

The more I read His Word, the more learn to be grateful for His love. I see every day that He loves me, because he shows me, even though I know I have not done the same. That is what makes me want to change the way that I treat others. Even if others do not treat me kindly and justly, I will continue to treat them as want to be treated.

Persistent Love

People will mistreat us and say hurtful things that seem to rip our feelings apart,

But we must forgive because Jesus forgives us, and gives us a new beginning and a fresh start.

Continue loving each other as you would want to be loved, This is not just m opinion, but a fact that comes from our Christ that s above.

Yes, it will get hard when we are pushed or when we get shoved; So pray to be given strength and to be humbled, and stay persistent in love.

Poem by Antonio E Walker

Way of Life

Dear Friends, let us continue to love one another, for love comes from God. Anyone who loves is a child of God and knows God.

BUT ANYONE WHO DOES not love does not know God, for God is Love.

1John 4:7-8
(NLT)

Prayer

Lord,

Thank you for your persistent love towards me. I know deep in m heart that you lead by example. Pease forgive me when I sometimes harden my heart toward others. Help me to stay strong in my love also.

Amen!

Chapter Six

Walking
In

Faith

For we walk by faith, not by sight.
2Corintians 5:7
(KJV)

Bread of Life

Now faith is the substance of all things hoped for, the evi-
dence of things not seen.

Hebrews 11:1
(KJV)

Released by Faith

A FRIEND OF MINE AND I used to cook up cocaine and sell t out of his house. His girlfriend really didn't like us selling from there, but she allowed t because she loved the money that he was making. I would cook the cocaine and turn it into crack rock. I never put any cut on it and had the best crack around. The fiends would come at all times of the night so that they could get the stuff.

They loved it and we had the whole hood sewed up.

While we waited on the customers, we would play video games and smoke on some green. One day I fell asleep and was awakened in the worst way, by the police. An officer told me to step outside where my friend was. I complied and did as I was told. When I got out of the door, I saw my homeboy sitting in a lawn chair surrounded by police officers. I was told to take a seat also.

When the officers asked my friend to consent to search his home, I was sure he would not give them permission. The officer promised that they would not take us to jail, no matter what they found inside. He said they would just confiscate any illegal contraband. I was shocked when my friend agreed and signed the consent.

The police found a couple sacks of marijuana, a sack of powder cocaine, a digital scale with residue on it, and a 9mm handgun. The officers came out of the house smiling and laughing. They handcuffed us and charged us both with possession of cocaine, use of a drug para-phernalia device, and possession of firearms a convicted felon.

My friend looked shocked and asked the officer why he had lied. The officer started laughing and ignored the question.

We were taken to jail. I was held without bond because I had a vi-olation of parole hold, but my friend made bond. I sat in jail for fif-teen months. During that time, I read the laws of possession. I learned that possession is nine-tenths of the law, meaning the substance had to actually be on your person or in your control. In order for a sub-

stance or item to be in your control, it had to be owned or rented in your name. I knew through common sense that I wasn't in possession or control of the house or the *drugs that where in it because it was all in his name.*

I was appointed a public attorney. He told me that the District Attorney was offering me ten straight years due to my prior convictions and drug history. He explained that if I went to trial and lost, I could receive up to thirty years. He said that if m friend decided to work with the DA and testify against me, I would lose. I went back to my dorm and prayed every day. I asked God to please have mercy on me.

My grandmother came to visit me. She knew my situation. I told her that I was scared and didn't know what to do. I explained to her that the law was on my side, but if my friend testified against me, I would lose. She told me to have faith in God and to walk in faith. She said that if I was going to pray, then I shouldn't worry, and if I was going to worry, then I shouldn't pray.

The following week, I went to court. When it was time for me to go in front of the judge, I got on my knees and thanked God for having mercy on me. I went into the courtroom and saw my homeboy. My heart started racing, but I told myself to have faith n God.

When the judge asked me how I wanted to plead, I told him not guilty. My friends plead guilty and told them that I was unaware of the illegal contraband found in his home. I couldn't believe it! I thanked God. A week later, my parole officer lifted the hold on me. My faith in God had freed me and sent me home.

If You Pray, Don't Worry

WALK IN FAITH AND NOT by sight,

Because if we are really trusting in God, then everything will be alright.

Whatever we ask for, if we have belief we will be able to receive.

All that is needed is persistent confidence and the choice to believe,

Jesus died for us and gave us the best gift that a friend can give, which is life.

So why doubt we will have anything that we ask for, when everything else comes up light.

If we depend on God for anything, He will take care of what we are in need of one day.

So if you are going to pray, don't worry; and if you are going to worry, don't *pray.*

Poem by Antonio E. Walker

Way of Life

Look at the lilies and how they grow. They don't work or make *their clothing, yet Solomon in all his glory was not dressed as beautifully as they are, And if God cares so wonderfully for*

flowers that are here today and thrown in the fire tomorrow, He

will certainly care for you. Why do you have so little faith?
Luke 12:27-28
(NLT)

Prayer:

Prayer of Faith
I arise today
Through a mighty strength:
God's power to guide me,
God's might to uphold me,
God's eyes to watch over me;
God's ear to hear me,
God's word to give me speech,
God's hand to guard me,
God's way to lie before me,
God's shield to shelter me,
God's host to secure me.
Amen

Chapter Seven

Protected Forever

Those Who trust in the Lord are as secure as Mount Zion;
They will not be defeated but will endure forever.

Psalm 125:1
(NLT)

Bread of Life

He that cometh to God must believe that He is, and that He
is a rewarder of them that diligently seek him.

Hebrews 11:6
(KJV)

Protected Forever

THE VERY FIRST DAY *at Smith State Prison, I was placed in a dorm that consisted of one hundred prisoners. These weren't your ordinary prisoners though. These were some of the most violent, destructive, and hostile prisoners in the state of Georgia. Smith State Prison is a level five, close security prison. It has the highest rate of stabbings and murders in the state of Georgia in each year. It is a disciplinary facility.*

I walked in the door and went into the room that I was assigned to. I was surprised at what I saw. There was a triple bunk bed that took up most of the room, a table, a sink and toilet, and three locker boxes on the wall. My two roommates introduced themselves. I unpacked y property and made up my bed. The room was so cramped that we could barely move around. I walked out of my room to get a little space.

I posted up on a wall to observe my surroundings. I noticed that there were a lot of gangs and organizations in the dorms. A couple of guys came up to me and asked where I was from. I told them Columbus. They said that I had a couple of homeboys in the dorm and called the other guys from Columbus over and introduced them to me.

One was an older guy that they called C-Town. He had been down for thirty-three years and was serving two life sentences. C-Town was what prisoners called a chain gang vet. He had been down for so long that he knew everything there was to know about prison. At first, I didn't really talk to him much but we *eventually became good friends.*

The other was a young guy named Zay. He was one of the head dudes of the gangsta disciples. Zay and I became close buddies from the first day. We liked doing the same kind of things- smoking weed, talking on the phone, and eating. We would chill all day together. After a couple of weeks, I learned that not only did Zay run the gansta disciples, but most of the dorm feared and respected him. Because I was his friend, everyone respected me also.

Sometimes, I would go and talk to C-Town. He was really into the Bible and kept his faith in God strong. When I would go to his room, C-Town was always reading the Bible or eating. He would give me a little o the Word and I would go back and hang with Zay.

I trusted and put my hope into Zay. I felt that he kept me safe and protected. Every day in Smith State Prison someone was getting stabbed, robbed, beaten, or killed. When I was with Zay, I didn't worry about anyone harming me because I knew he had my back.

One day, someone stole eleven ramen noodle soups from a Mexican prisoner. The Mexicans stuck together. They all went around asking if anyone had seen or knew who had stolen the noodles. No one said anything and they went back to their rooms. I assumed that they were just going to leave the issue alone.

A few minutes later, Zay and I heard someone scream and ran to see what was going on. A group of Mexicans where running around stabbing people. One of them rushed by me with a shank, but didn't stab me. The guards came in with shields and masks and resolved the situation. The warden came and gave orders to lock everyone down inside our assigned rooms. Then they came and questioned all of the Mexicans and the gansta disciples. Someone had told the warden that one of the ganstas had stolen the soups. All of the gansta disciples, even Zay, were moved to another dorm. I was afraid. Zay was gone and now I had no one to help me.

I went and talked to C-Town. I told him that I was going to leave the dorm. I explained that Zay was gone and I was all alone. C-Town explained to me that God and Jesus were the only ones who had been protecting me. He told me that I had put my hope into the wrong person. He said that I should trust God and ask Him to protect me.

I honestly believed that He would, and He did. I never needed or had a shank or other weapon. The only thing I had was my Bible *and my faith in God and Jesus to keep me safe and alive. I read Psalm 125:1 and knew that was going to be alright and protected forever.*

He Will Care for Us

We should give our cares and burdens to Jesus and He will protect us during our fights.

If we are blind and we trust in Him, with His love He will give us sight.

Facing obstacles and people who stand and try to bring us down, He will be our fortress, our savior, and our shelter on steady ground.

Give Him all our worries and call anytime we are in need of rest, **If we don't believe He will help us, then try Him and believe** *because* **He will pass the test.**

Our Lord is with us and thank the almighty God for that.

And if we ever face any trouble or danger he will take care of us. This is not only the truth, but also a fact.

Poem by Antonio E Walker

Way of Life

So humble yourselves under the mighty power of God, and at the right time he will lift you up in honor. Give all your worries and cares to God, for he cares about you.
1Peter 5:6-7
(NLT)

Prayer

*Almighty Father God,
I put my trust in You, and only in You and Your Son Jesus*

Christ. I love you Lord and thank You for providing me with everything I need. I Have faith that You will do everything for

me that You said that You would do in Your Word. Therefore, I will never doubt and will stand firm in my belief.

Amen!

Chapter Eight

There

is a
Reason

And in very deed for this cause have I raised thee up, for to shew in thee my power; and that my name may be declared throughout all the earth.
Exodus 9:16
(KJV)

Bread of Life

*Salvation is not a reward for the good things we have done,
so* none of us can boast about it... For we are God's mas-
terpiece.

*He created us anew in Christ Jesus, so we can do the good
things he planned for us long ago.*

Ephesians 2:9-10
(NLT)

There is a Reason

THE FIRST TIME I RAN away was while my mom was serving time for drug possession. I was living with my grandmother's brother, my *great-uncle. He was a very heavy drinker and would always bring up the past whenever he got drunk. I had stolen a rare con from him when I was five. Even though I was then ten, he threw it up in my face a lot.*

After about a month, I got fed up and didn't return to his house after school. Instead, I went to my friend Eric's house. Eric *had a big family. He asked his mom if I could stay with them. She asked me why I had run away. I gave her my reasons.* Eric's mother said that if my uncle gave her permission, I could *stay at her home until my mother got out of jail.*

Eric's mother, Ms.Katie as I called her, drove me back to *my* uncle's house and knocked on the door. She introduced herself and *stated why she had come. To my surprise, my uncle had not been* drinking and said that he didn't care. I happily got my things *and said goodbye to my sisters.*

For the most part, everyone in the family accepted me. I liked living with them. Eric and I told everyone at school that we were cousins. Ms. Katie was a very kind and open-hearted woman; she took me in even though she was not able to get any financial assistance to help her take care of me. She did it strictly from the kindness of her heart.

We went to church Sunday and spent time as a family throughout the week. Ms. Katie was one of the best cooks I have ever known in my life. There is an old saying, "She put her foot in it". *Well, Ms. Katie put her whole leg into it.*

*I only stayed with them for about a year. But I learned so much from her. When my mom got out of jail, I was conflicted. I didn't re*ally want to leave my new family, but I missed my mom *and sisters* *as well. I still sometimes went and spent the night with Eric and his family, but I eventually moved and lost contact.*

Some time later, I was living on m own. One of my homeboys and I were walking to the store to buy some cigars when a van swerved up on us. At first, I thought that it was the police. I thought of running, but then I saw that it was Ms. Katie and some of her granddaughters. She asked me how I was doing and I said I was OK. She told me that she was sick from time to time. I said that I hoped she felt better and we said our goodbyes. I didn't think that would be the last time I saw Ms. *Katie, but it was.*

It was years later and I was in jail the next time I saw Eric. When I saw him walk into the dorm I was in, I walked over to him and we embraced. We caught up on what had been going on in each other's lives. He looked sad when I asked him how Ms. *Kate was doing. I knew what he was going to say – that she had passed away. I told him that I was sorry to hear that and I really was.*

I now think about all of the wonderful and kind people that god has put into my life. I have always been a strong believer that God puts people into our lives for a reason, whether it is for a second, a minute, or a lifetime. He put Ms. Katie into my life and everyone else that has helped me in one way or another. I just want to thank God for His fa-vor and say that we should always be careful how we treat people be-cause you never know why God has placed us in one another's lives. **But you can always know for** *sure that there is a reason.*

There is a Reason

There is a reason the sun shines in the day and then at night the moon,

Our children are allowed to play their games and have fun in the light, but the dark brings out raccoons.

There is a reason the birds fly south in the winter and frogs hop n the spring,

Leaves will turn brown and die in the fall and in the summertime there are new ones that are green.

There is a reason that people come into our lives whether it is for a second, a minute, or an hour.

Maybe the reason is to help us get through a difficult situation or to show us that God can work in anybody, because He controls the whole world with His wisdom, might, and power.

Poem by Antonio E Walker

Way of Life

And we know that all things work together for good to them that love God, to them who are the called according to his purpose.

Romans 8:28
(KJV)

prayer

Chapter Nine

God Can Use Anyone

DON'T COPY THE BEHAVIOR and customs of this world, but let God *transform you into a new person by changing the way you think.* Then you will learn to know God's will for you, which is good and *pleasing and perfect.*

*Romans 12:2
(NLT)*

Bread of Life

When a potter makes jars out of clay, doesn't he have the right to *use the same lump of clay to make one jar for decoration and another to throw garbage into?*

Romans 9:21
(NLT)

God Can Use Anyone

ONE OF MY DEAREST FRIENDS growing up was a guy named Rahaiem. When I first met him, times were hard for my family and me. My mom was just begging to use drugs and we had just moved into a very bad neighborhood. I was accustomed to being the worst kid in predominantly white schools, but now I was attending a school that was 90% black. I had a lot of competition.

On the first night in our new home, I remember being awakened by gunshots. I was a little frightened because, before then, I had only heard gunshots on TV. The next day, my mother told me to go out and play somewhere. So I walked around the neighborhood taking in the sights.

This section of town was totally different than anywhere I'd lived *before. My mom had always tried to keep us out of the projects and high crime areas. We had always stayed in low-income houses, but in middle class neighborhoods. The people in this area were mostly black people who were having a hard time, just like my family.*

I met Rahaiem when I walked past his house. He and his brothers were playing Power Rangers. I used to love the Power Rangers and anything that had to do with martial arts. I stopped to watch them playing and when Rahaiem asked if I wanted to play, I said yes. From that point on we became inseparable. Rahaiem also had four sisters, so my sisters would come and play with them. His family took to our family pretty quickly. His mom and dad saw that we were very mannerable. We respected adults and did what we were told. They knew by our clothes that we were poor. When they saw our house and found out that our mom was hooked on drugs, they sort of adopted us in a way. Whatever Rahaiem and his family did, they included us. We never really stayed at our own house.

Rahaiem's family was more fortunate than everyone else in the neighborhood. His father was a big-time drug dealer and club owner.

Rahaiem's *family took us shopping and out to eat. I* know that Rahaiem's dad probably felt that he was giving back because he showed us so much love. My sisters and I didn't know that drugs were being sold out of the house. Rahaiem's dad never *let us see him doing anything illegal. I just thought he was a millionaire. /I really looked up to him and saw him as the father* I'd never had and always appreciated the kindness he showed to *my sisters and me.*

Rahaiem's father is out of the drug game now and never got *caught selling drugs. Now all he does s run his cubs. People will* always be quick to judge others. They don't look at their own wrong doings but will put someone else's on display. I have heard some same that Rahaiem's dad is a disgrace to society and th*at he is a low*-down person. My opinion is that only God's opinion matters. At one of my family's lowest points in life, Rahaiem's *dad helped us on many occasions. I also know that he hurt families by selling drugs, but we all sin in some shape or fashion. So whoever feels that their opinions about another matters, let he or she who is without sin cast the first stone because God can use anyone.*

Never Question God

No matter how we feel about a person or what kind of sins the may have done,

The Lord uses who He pleases and anything that is under the sun.

We are only on this earth to carry out His divine purpose. If ever we become confused, wondering what the true meaning of life is, just pray to God and His plans will come to the surface.

He created the heavens and everything that is underneath it. Through His wisdom He gave us a brain to understand mysteries and a nose to breathe with.

He sacrificed His only begotten son Jesus Christ so that all people will have a chance to be redeemed.

And even though we may think that someone is too wicked to be used, remember we are never to question God and things are not always what they seem.

Poem by Antonio E Walker

Way of Life

THUS SAITH THE LORD, the Holy one of Israel, and his maker, Ask me of things to come concerning my sons, and concerning the work

> *of my hands command ye me. I have made the earth, and created man upon it: I even my hands, have stretched out the heavens, and all their host have I commanded.*
> *Isaiah 45:11-12*
> *(KJV)*

Prayer

Chapter Ten

All
About Self

Whoever gives to the poor will lack nothing, but those who close their eyes to poverty will be cursed.
Proverbs 28:27
(NLT)

Bread of Life

OH, THE JOYS OF THOSE who are kind to the poor! The Lord rescues them when they are in trouble. The Lord protects them and keeps them alive. He gives them prosperity in the land and rescues them from their enemies. The Lord nurses them when they are sick and restores them to health.

Psalms 41:1-3
(NLT)

Looking out for Myself

When you have thousands of dollars saved, but your family goes without and struggles to make ends meet, then you should consider yourself a very, very selfish person. I am not one to judge others because I sin and have been lost in deception myself. I have had my own faults and shortcomings throughout life. It took prison, the chance to get off drugs and clear my mind, to come to this conclusion. I have three sisters who grew up just like I did, in poverty. When I started making money selling drugs, I could have easily given them money. Instead, I stayed away from them because I knew they would give the money to my mom.

As I got older, I couldn't blame my mother for my selfishness *anymore. My sisters had begun living on their own and having children. One of them is a very ambitious and has used where we came from as a motivation to get into the medical field. She has a son and has been attending college for nine years now. Unlike me, she has always tried to help my other sisters and my mom.*

She has a kind and generous heart for my nieces and nephews. She struggled just like I did coming up, but unlike me, she stayed with my mom and sisters when I left.

Me, on the other hand, I knew that my other siblings were struggling and because I had so much selfishness in my heart, all I cared about was myself. I don't have any kids and bought *myself the things I wanted.*

I never even bought anyone in my family anything for birthdays or Christmas. If I happened to run across them in the streets, I would sometimes give them twenty or thirty dollars. I felt justified because of my feelings toward them, but when I look back now, I feel very ashamed of how I treated them.

To this day I really don't know my sisters, nieces or nephews. I *think back on all* that we endured, and I hate that I didn't help *them* when I had the money. That is one of my goals now- to stop being self-centered and selfish.

I didn't always believe that I was selfish. I really thought that I was a kind and giving person. There have been many times that I have helped or given money to other people. Even so, I now realize that the only times that I have given are those times that I have received or expected something in return.

A woman could ask me for money or for clothes for her kids, and I wouldn't even think twice about it, but my motive was to have sex with her or to impress her. My youngest sister has five kids, and it saddens me to say that I have never bought them any clothes or shoes. I haven't even spent any time with them. All I have done was tell them that I love them, but never shown them love in my actions.

My mom has been homeless many times. My sisters, even though they were struggling themselves, always let her come and stay with them. I, on the other hand, had the money to put her in a townhouse and would not have missed the money. My daily expenses totaled $550. I spent all that money on things for which I benefited nothing. Meanwhile, my mom was living at someone else's house because I would not forgive her for things that had happened eighteen years before.

That is one of the main reasons that I think that I am in prison.

I know that selling drugs is wrong, but if I would have done more to help others or my own family, maybe God would have been more lenient toward me.

Selfish Ambitions

God loves a person who bountifully and generously gives to the poor,

He puts upon them blessings and takes their substance and multiplies it more.

He has great favor for those who are kind to people who are without,

If we see anther hungry, we are to give them some food to put in their mouth.

Maybe someone is homeless, cold and tired;

Then we should give them a place to rest because to whom much is given, much s required.

Every day is a test to see if we will do our part, because God looks down on all of us from heaven to see if anyone truly has a giving heart.

So we should forget about ourselves and not lose sight of our missions,

And live to serve others instead of focusing on our own selfish ambitions.

Poem by Antonio E Walker

Way of Life

He which soweth sparingly shall reap also sparingly; and he which soweth bountifully shall reap also bountifully. Every man according as he purposeth in his heart, so let him give; not grudgingly, or of necessity: for God loveth a cheerful giver.

2Corinthians 9:6-7
(KJV)

Prayer

Chapter Eleven

The

Rich Get Richer

YOU KNOW THE GENEROUS grace of the Lord Jesus Christ. Though He was rich, yet for your sake he became poor, so that by His poverty He could make you rich.

2 Corinthians 8:9

(NLT)

Bread of Life

The rich and the poor have this in common: The Lord made them both.

Proverbs 22:2 (NLT)

Testimony

Don't Lean on *Uncertain Riches*

IF WE ONLY GIVE TO the rich how can we say that we are followers of Jesus Christ?

To close our eyes and turn our heads on people who are poor will cause God's wrath to ignite.

It is easier for a camel to slide through a needle's eye than for a *wealthy man or woman to obtain eternal life.*

So don't put off helping someone until the morning if we are *capable of giving it to them tonight.*

Loving only because we are loved is not hard at all, But to love when we aren't loved in return is how the Godly are *able to stand tall.*

To lean on uncertain riches is like leaning on air,

And if you think they will be able to save you, then you better be prepared.

Poem by Antonio E Walker

Way of Life

Charge them that are rich in this world, that they be not highminded, nor trust in uncertain riches, but in the living God, who

giveth all things to enjoy; That they do good, that they be rich n good works, ready to distribute, willing to communicate.

1 Timothy 6:17-18
(KJV)

Prayer

Lord Jesus,
I PRAY TO YOU ASKING for forgiveness of my sins. Lord I have been trusting n money and other worldly things to make me happy.

I haven't treated others like I would want to be treated. I have *put myself, my desires, and my wants before You and everyone*

else. I am sorry Lord and I thank you for showing me that the riches in this world will rot away, but the riches that are in heaven will last forever.

Amen!

Chapter Twelve

Sick and Tired of Being Sick and Tired

Come to me, all e who labour and are heavy laden, and I will give you rest.

Matthew 11:28
(KJV)

Bread of Life

ALL PRAISE TO GOD THE father of our Lord Jesus Christ. God is our merciful Father and the source of all comfort, He comforts us in all our troubles so that we can comfort others. When they are troubled, we will be able to give them the same comfort God has given us.
2 Corinthians 1:3-4
(NLT)

Sick and Tired of Being Sick and Tired

Growing up with two sisters was very challenging for me. I was the oldest and it was my job to stand up for them. If something or some-one tried to harm them, I had to try to protect them. Being that I was the only boy, I had to play a lot of games that girls like. My sisters' favorite games were playing house, playing *with dolls, and hide and go seek. To be honest some of them were also my favorites.*

There were also some benefits to growing up n an all female household, especially when you are a manly little boy like I was. My sisters had plenty of girls over a lot. Sometimes they would spend the night. Since I was always playing with my sisters, I got to play with their friends too. Since I was the only boy, I was automatically the dad when we played house, the doctor of sick dolls, and the seeker of hide and seek.

I was never really bored, but I did get tired of always playing their games; and since my mom was not able to have more kids, my sisters were my brothers also. I made them play all the games I liked too. We played karate, hunting, football, and kickball. If I got mad at them I would try to beat them up, but they were smart and would usually jump me. Since it would be four on one, including my mom, I didn't have a chance at coming out as the *victor.*

I really loved my sisters and as I am writing this I feel a lot of mixed emotions - feelings of regret, shame, sadness, and happiness. I hate that I did not have the will or determination to stay with them through their struggles. I was so tired of not having what other kids had, luxuries like hot water, electricity, food, clean clothes, and a stable home.

When my mom went to jail the second time, I went to foster care. I found out that I didn't have to live the way I had with my *mom.*

No foster parent could put their hands on me or curse at me. The state supplied a weekly allowance and clothing vouchers. The first time that I had new name brand shoes was when I was in foster care. It was one of the best feelings I had as a child. I decided never to go back and stay with my mom again. These things I had decided to have rather than my sisters and my mom.

What made me really regret my decision was a tragic incident that happened to one of my sisters. My sister had become friends with a girl she knew at school. After school, she would go to her friend's house and chill. Sometimes, she would spend the night at *her house on the weekends. Her mom worked most of the time. The girl was fast and would have a lot of different boys over. One night, while my sister was there, four boys came over. Her friend liked one of the boys and told my sister that she wanted to have sex with him. She asked my sis-ter if she liked any of the* other boys. My sister said she didn't. My sis-ter's friend asked *her to just chill with the other boys. After her friend left, one of the boys pushed my sister down. Although my sister fought back, the boy went crazy, punching her like she was a man. He ended up beating her up badly. When my sister told me this, my blood began boiling, but what could I do? The incident had taken place when she was thirteen, many years before I found out about it. I wished that I had been there to protect and defend her, but I* wasn't there. I'd al-ready left because I was sick and tired of *being sick and tired.*

Sick and Tired of Being Sick and Tired

CAST THY BURDENS ON the Lord and be persistent to the end, Fore we all have hard times without any help, not even from our friends.

Some of us will give up hope and look for the first opportunity to flee,

But keep yourself in place because you have a powerful God that is with thee.

It will be very difficult believing that things are better this way, But there is something that is to be learned and taken from each and every day.

So take the good and the bad and live life with plenty of zest, Because when we are sick and tired of being sick and tired, the Lord will give us a place that we can go to rest.

Poem by Antonio E Walker

Way of Life

Cast thy burden upon the Lord, and he shall sustain thee: he shall never suffer the righteous to be moved.

Psalm 55:22
(KJV)

Prayer

Chapter Thirteen

A Just Judge

AND THIS IS WHAT THE Lord says: If the innocent must suffer, how much more must you! You will not go unpunished! You must drink the cup of judgment!

Jeremiah 49:12

(NLT)

Bread of Life

FOR THE LORD WILL NOT cast off for ever; but though he cause grief, yet will he have compassion according to the multitude of his mercies. For he doth not afflict willingly nor grieve the children of men.

Lamenations 3:31-33

(KJV)

Perverted Games

Children should always be carefully watched when they are growing up. There are many predators and perverted men, women and even other children who prey on their innocence. There are hundreds of thousands of kids who are molested, raped, kidnapped, and killed every year. Children are very smart, but they are also very vulnerable and can easily be tricked into dong things that are unacceptable. The predators make them think that they are playing games. They offer prizes like candy, toys, money, or food to get the children to do what they want.

When a child is violated, the experience stays with them and affects them mentally, physically, and socially for the rest of their lives. Some are abused at such a young age that they don't even *remember the things that have happened to them. Others carry the pain, burden and grief around with them.*

One of my sisters and I were abused when we were young. I am not sure s she remembers it because she was only three years old at the time. I was five and I remember it like it happened yesterday. The incident has affected me emotionally. I think that it was also one of the reasons that I chose to leave my mother and sisters. I was always very uncomfortable when my sister and I were close or touched. I didn't feel the same about my other *sisters. I tried to avoid being around her alone. If we had to* ride in a car together, I didn't want to be near her. Sometimes I *had to sit beside her and, with four of us n the back seat, it was impossible to not touch each other. If her leg touched mine, I hated it* with all of my heart. I don't think that my sister had the *same feelings because she never flinched up in disgust like I did when we touched.*

I don't remember the guy that abused us, but I do hate that I *remember what he made my sister and I do. This is the first time I have told anyone except my mother this story.*

At the time, we were living next to a guy that was a friend of my mother's. He was a white guy, but my mom has never been *prejudice* *and taught my sisters and me to love everyone the same. He would* *help us with food and other things that we needed whenever he could.* *My mom trusted this guy and would let my oldest sister and I go to his* *house and play.*

One day when we were at his house, he asked us if we wanted a *peanut butter and jelly sandwich. We both loved peanut butter and* *jelly sandwiches, so we quickly said yes. He made a sandwich and gave* *us both half. I remember being a little disappointed that* I didn't get a whole sandwich, but I didn't say anything because I didn't want to *seem greedy. When finished our halves, he asked us if we wanted a* *whole sandwich. I thought that he was a mind reader. Excitedly we* *told him yes.*

He told us he would give us a whole sandwich if we took our *clothes* off. We didn't know any better so *we did what he told us to* *do. We sat at the table and waited for him to fix our sandwiches. It* *was a little awkward sitting there naked, but there was no way I was* *going to mess up getting m peanut butter and jelly sandwich. He gave* *us our sandwiches and we ate them quickly.*

He told us that he would make us another one if we played a game with him. He said that we couldn't tell anyone and, if we did, he wouldn't give us any more candy or sandwiches. We told him that we wouldn't tell.

He told my sister to get on the bed and lay down. When she did, *he picked me up and put me on top of her. He kept trying to make us* *do weird stuff to each other until I started to cry. He got scared and* *told me he would fix me another sandwich if I would stop. He told us* *to put our clothes back on and fixed the sandwiches. While we ate, he* *made us promise again that we would not tell anyone.*

I told my mom. The guy denied it, but she called the police. They didn't do anything to the guy. I hate to think about *all of* the times that we went to play with him that I don't remember or *know what he did to us. But I know that God knows and I know that God will judge all of us justly.*

Perverted Games

Everyone n this world is not to be trusted with our kids, And just because we think someone had our best interests in mind, doesn't mean that they really did.

People can deceive us and have wicked motives hidden in their mind,

*And just because they hel*ped us once, doesn't mean they will do it *each and every time.*

Our children are very precious and must be safe and protected with all of our might,

Because there are a lot of dangerous people trying to hurt them but they are too small to defend themselves or fight.

So keep a watchful eye on them. Their safety is to be maintained Because there are a lot of sick people in the world who like to play perverted games.

Poem by Antonio E Walker

Way of Life

So obey my instructions, and do not defile yourselves by committing
any of these detestable practices that were committed by the people
who lived in the land before you. I am the Lord your God.
Leviticus 18:30
(NLT)

Prayer

Father God,
There have been many times n my life when I felt you weren't by my side. I have wondered why others seem to be able to do things

to me and get away with hurting me. Lord I now understand that you allow things to happen to me to strengthen me for your will

that you have put me on this earth to do. I do not trust in anyone or anything else because I now know that you are the only wise and just judge. So from now on, no matter what I face or have to go through, I will keep my hope and faith n you.

Amen!

Chapter Fourteen

Protected by

Grace

The Lord is good, a strong hold in the day of trouble; and he knoweth them that trust him.

Nahum 1:7
(KJV)

Bread of Life

Though he fall, he shall not be utterly cast down: for the Lord upholdeth him with his hand.

Psalms 37:24
(KJV)

Protected by Grace

I REMEMBER WATCHING my mom dating when I was growing up. I used to get jealous of the men that were taking her out. She would always dress up and look real pretty for them. When her date arrived, we would meet him and later she would ask us what we thought of him. I never liked any of them. My sisters used to like some of them, but I felt rejected. I wanted to be the only male in her life. I didn't trust any man having seen the way my sister's *dad beat my mom up. I figured that was what all men did to women – beat them when they felt they needed it.*

Every time my mom left to go out with a man, I wondered if she would come back. When she did return, t would be after midnight. We were supposed to go to bed at nine PM, but I always stayed up until she got home. I couldn't sleep, so I would turn on the *TV and wait. When she saw that I was up, she would just say that I had better go to sleep so that I could be up for school in the* morning. I'd give her a hug and a kiss and go to sleep happy *knowing that she had made it home safely.*

I knew about God and Jesus at a very early age. My mom sent my sisters and me to church on Wednesdays and Sundays. I used to pray and ask God to protect my mom and bring her home safely. I really didn't know what I w*as doing, but I remembered that, in* church, the children's' preacher used to tell us that God would *answer us when we prayed to him. So that was what I believed and did.*

My mom also had quite a few female friends who would come over to the house. I liked all of her female friends. Some of them would say I was cute and that I looked like the singer Babyface. I didn't know Babyface was, but I guessed that he was someone *that women liked. When my mom and her friends would drink or smoke marijuana, they would laugh and act silly. I thought that* they were funny so I'd laugh.

I still like being around women to this day, but I do not feel comfortable around men. I know that there are a lot of slimy and dishonest women in this world, but if I had m choice of their company or that of cutthroat men, I would choose the ladies every time.

Sometimes, my mom would go out on a double date with one of her female friends. On one of these occasions, my mom was going out to the Fort Benning military base with one of her best friends.

The woman had met a soldier who had a friend who was available.

My mom, not being the type to pass up a chance to meet Mr. Right, agreed to the set-up.

My mom's friend came to our house to get ready. They both *looked really pretty. The soldiers showed up at about 8:30 and, to my surprise, one of them was a white guy. I think that my mom was surprised too, but she said nothing. She told me to make sure that my sisters behaved. She kissed us and left. When 2:00 came and she still was not home, I started to worry a* little. My sisters were asleep, but I couldn't lie down. My mom didn't get home until around 3:30. When she came into the *house, I saw the police driving off and she was crying.*

My mom said that the soldiers had taken them to dinner and then to a club, where they drank and danced until about 1:30. The soldiers took them back to the base and refused to take them home until they had sex with them. When my mom and her friend refused, they tried to force themselves on them. My mom said that she fought the white guy and hit him in the head with a lamp. His friend punched her in the back of the head and burned her on the face with a cigarette. My mom's friend was able to go get *some other soldiers to help them. Luckily, my mom and her friend were able to escape with only a few cuts and bruises. The two soldiers were locked up and charged with attempted rape and aggravated assault.*

After hearing all of this, I hugged my mom and silently thanked God for protecting her through His love, mercy, and grace. God had helped her n her time of need.

God is Everywhere

When we feel that there is no help and we are about to fall, do not worry because God is there.

Times may be tough, and we are in a bind, but do not worry because God is there.

Maybe we are being pursued or cornered with no place to go, but do not worry because God is there.

We may be lost in the woods or trapped in the snow, but do not worry because God is there.

People will try to harm us and bring us down, but do not worry because God is there.

Distress might fall on us and there is no one around, but do not worry because God is omnipresent and our God is everywhere.

Poem by Antonio E Walker

Way of Life

So let us come boldly to the throne of our gracious God. There we will receive his mercy, and we will find grace to help us when we need it most.

Hebrews 4:16 (NLT)

Praye

Chapter Fifteen

God's
Guardian Angels

The Lord of Heaven's Armies s here among us; the God of Israel *is*
our fortress.
Psalm 46:7
(NLT)

Bread of Life

BECAUSE THOU HAST MADE the Lord, which s my refuge, even
the most high, thy habitation; There shall no evil befall thee, neither
shall any plague come nigh thy dwelling. For he shall give his angels
charge over thee, to keep thee in thy ways.
Psalm 91:9-11
(KJV)

Protected by God

One Saturday night, I went over to my homeboy's house to chill with him and play video games. He had a 62" TV, so it *enhanced the visual and audio features. I have always loved playing video games, especially sports games. That night started off like any other. At first we played Call of Duty and Grand Theft Auto. Then we moved on to football and basketball games. I was really good and very hard to beat. My friends used to call me a game freak because all that I ever wanted to do was sell dope and play video games.*

On this night, time went by quickly and, before I knew it, it was 1:30 in the morning. We were hungry but didn't have a car, so *we had to wait until someone with a ride showed up. At about 2:30, a girl showed up to buy some marijuana. We asked her if she would take us up the street to get something to eat. I had a taste for some Waffle House, and tried to get her to take us there. She said that she was in a hurry because she had stolen the car from her mom and had to get it back before her mother woke up. She agreed to take me to the service station.*

When the girl and I got into the car, I noticed a crack head's car *riding by the house. I figured that he wanted some crack. I had some, but, at the time, I was only interested in getting something to eat. At the store, I bought some hotdogs, chips, sodas, and a gallon of milk. I paid for the stuff and hopped back into the car with the girl. Because she was in a hurry, she dropped me off a* few houses down from my friend's house. *I paid her five dollars and started walking.*

As I walked, the same crack head rode by me again. I whistled and he stopped. When I walked up to the car, I noticed that there was a woman driving and two men were with her. The front passenger and back doors opened and the men jumped out. One of them had a steel baseball bat and the other had a crowbar.

I took off running but the man with the bat cornered me at a fence. He tried to swing and hit me with the bat, but I caught the bat with both hands and we began to struggle for control of it. We fell to the ground wrestling. By this time, the guy with the crowbar had caught up to us. I screamed for help. The guy hit me in the leg with the crowbar. I was rolling around on the ground trying to hold the first guy, while dodging the second guy. The crack head on the ground yelled for the other to hit me in the head. The guy hesitated, I think because he was afraid that he would kill me. As he raised the crowbar to bash me in the head, a light beamed on us. It was the sheriff.

That was the happiest I had ever been to see the police. I don't *know where he came from, but I do know that God had an angel* protecting me for sure. I can't even imagine what would have happened if God hadn't put that sheriff on *that street that morning. I know that those guys probably would have killed me, but God rescued me. I look back and I thank and praise His Holy name for having a guardian angel watching over me.*

The God of Heaven's Armies

GOD ORDERS HIS ANGELS to protect us and tells them that our feet need to not scrub the ground.

The passionate affection that He has for us can nowhere else be found.

We are His prize possessions, protected better than money that is held in a bank vault.

Many people have ridiculed and slandered our reputations, but to Him, we have no faults.

Evil thoughts and wicked plans against us will never be carried about.

The devil may be close to trapping us, but Jesus will show us a way out.

When we are outnumbered and in fear all we can do is shout. But do not be afraid because God and Hs armies in heaven will give us protection and fight and win the bout.

Poem by Antonio E Walker

Way of Life

He will order his angels to protect you. And they will hold you up with their hands so you won't even hurt your foot on a stone.

Matthew 4:6
(NLT)

Prayer

Thank You God for always being there when I have needed You the most. The love that You have for me is undeserved. I am so

grateful for the grace and mercy that You give me. Every day I wake up, You have a stronghold for me and my family sending

your angels to protect us from harm. I love You and ask that You continue to bless me with Your presence in my life.

Amen!

Chapter Sixteen

Blinded by

Rage

But now is the time to get rid of anger, rage, malicious behavior, slander, and dirty language.

Colossians 3:8 (NLT)

Bread of Life

Stop being angry! Turn from your rage!

Do not lose your temper – it only leads to harm.

Psalm 37:8
(NLT)

Filled with Anger

WATCHING MY MOTHER getting beat up by my youngest sister's dad *made me want to kill him, but I was a child and he was an adult. All I could do was call the police. It made me even angrier that every time she had him locked up, she would take him back when he got out of jail. I started thinking and believing that this was how women wanted to be treated. I have never been the type of man that beats on women, but I have slapped or hit a woman on a few occasions.*

There was one incident that I got so furious with a woman that I did become extremely violent. At the time, the girl and I had been going together. I went to jail and she got pregnant while I was locked up. When I got out, we started dating again. I accepted her little boy as my own because I loved her and wanted to be with her. I still had a lot of bottled up anger toward her for getting pregnant, but I thought that the feelings were manageable.

One night, we went to the club together and began arguing. I had been drinking and was nearly intoxicated. She left the club with some of her homegirls and I got one of my homeboys to take me to follow her. She and her friends pulled into a gas station. I got out of my friend's car and walked to the car she was in.

Earlier at the club, while we were arguing, she had called me an orphan child. She didn't know it, but those words, with the help *of the alcohol, had infuriated me. I wanted to kill her. When the girl saw me, she jumped out of the car and stood up to me like I was joking and playing. I slapped her and she swung back. I then grabbed her by her hair and started punching her. A truck driver told me to leave her alone, which I did for a couple of seconds. She had run into the store, thinking that I would not follow her. She was wrong.*

I was so filled with alcohol and anger that I went into the store like I owned it. There were a lot of people on the store that had wit-

nessed us fighting outside. The girl ran behind the counter where she thought she was safe. The store clerk told me to leave and that the police were on the way.

Most people would have left, but not me, not that day. Instead, I picked up every glass bottle that I could get my hands on and threw them at her. People started running and screaming. The girl ducked behind the counter and the store clerk ran into the bathroom.

When I ran out of bottles, I started throwing candy bars and ice creams. I stopped long enough to notice that the store had cleared out. Something inside of me told me to leave. I walked out of the store calmly and got back into my friend's car and we left.

It didn't stop there though. The girl had a car that her baby's *daddy had bought for her. She loved that little car. She had* left it at her friend's house before going to the club earlier that day. I told my homeboy to take me to her friend's house. When we got there, I destroyed the car with a chair that was sitting outside.

After that, I felt much better and went back to the club. I had released all of the pent up anger. The next morning, I woke up sober and thought about the things I'd done the *night before. I was ashamed, shocked, and scared. I was on parole, and I knew for a fact that I had just sent myself back to prison.*

By the grace of God, I didn't go back to jail. When the people at *the gas station had asked the girl who I was, she gave them a fake name. She called me and said that I had better get her car fixed or she would give them my real name. I got her car fixed and eventually, we started dating each other again. I made a promise to myself that from that day forth, I would never drink or put my hands on another woman as long as I lived.*

Way of Life

He that s slow to anger is better than the mighty; and he that ruleth his spirit than he who taketh a city.
Proverbs 16:32
(KJV)

A Humbled Heart

WE HAVE TO BE UNDERSTANDING towards the people that we meet, Because they will do and say things that will make us want to retreat.

Sometimes instead of retreating we will want to stay and fight, But be gentle and stay calm to keep from giving your temper a delight.

Focus on Jesus and the words to us that He left –

To turn the other cheek and to continue to love them as we continue to love our self.

So when you get mad and would like to tear someone apart, Take a deep breath and let the Lord intervene and humble your heart.

Poem by Antonio E Walker

Prayer

Chapter Seventeen

Hot Temperature

An angry person starts fights; A hot tempered person commits all kinds of sins.
Proverbs 29:22
(NLT)

Bread of Life

Control your temper, for anger labels you a fool.
Ecclesiastes 7:9
(NLT)

Blinded by Rage

WHILE SERVING TIME in prison, I met a man named Deandre. We called him Dee for short. I had been going to church services and had noticed him there also. You have to be very careful of the prisoners that you befriend; but after spending some tie with Dee, I learned that he was a very caring and kind person. If someone was hungry and Dee had food n his locker, he would give it to them without hesitation, even if it was his last. We ended up becoming good friends and encouraged each other to stay persistent and strong while trying to better ourselves and serve God. The more time that we spent together, the closer we became.

Dee was very talented at cutting hair. He cut my hair and most everyone else's in the dorm. He charged a reasonable price and would even give haircuts to the inmates who were not fortunate enough to have commissary to pay him.

One of the reasons that Dee and I became so close was because we had similar backgrounds. Dee had also been in the drug game and used to make a lot of money on the streets. He had been more advanced and at a higher level in the game than me. At the time, I thought that I would go back to selling drugs when I got back out into the free world, so I used to soak up everything that he told me.

Dee had a cousin in Atlanta that was a millionaire. He used to get kilos of pure cocaine from his cousin. Dee would take the pure coke back to his small town of Newnan, Georgia where it was the best thing floating around. He could cut it a few times and it was still better than anything anyone else had in town. Dee said that he made money that way so easily that he didn't have to sell *his cocaine like other dealers who had to get in the streets and compete. People came looking for him.*

The more Dee told me about his connection for the pure cocaine, the more I wanted to be a part of his team. I would daydream about *getting some of that coke and taking it back to Columbus. Every day I would ask Dee for his information and phone number, but he* would get quiet and give me no answer. Because I didn't want to *be a pest, I would let it go for the day.*

One day, Dee told me why he couldn't give me his information. *He said that he was not in prison for drugs, but for murder. At first I thought that he was playing. There was no way that this kind and gentle man had murdered anyone. Then Dee told me his story.*

Dee was 36 years old and had married his wife when he was 27. She was only 21 at the time and one of the finest women in the area. When Dee first laid eyes on her, he fell in love and couldn't *think about anything but making her his wife. Every day he perused her and every day she turned him down. He bought her whatever she wanted and, eventually, she gave in and they became a couple.*

A year later, she became pregnant with their first and only child. They soon got married and Dee thought that his life was perfect. They had a big house, cars, clothes, and jewelry. The only times that they were apart were when Dee went out of town to get more cocaine. He would usually stay for a day or two and return back to Newnan.

One time, he did not stay overnight in Atlanta, but came right back home. Dee said that when he opened his front door, he heard sounds coming from his bedroom. When he opened the bedroom door, he saw his wife and his best friend having sex. After that his mind went blank and he was filled with rage.

Dee always took his gun with him when he went to Atlanta, so he still had it on his waist. He drew the gun and emptied the clip killing both his wife and friend. When he calmed down and realized what he had done, he took his daughter, who had been sleeping, to his mom's house and went to the police.

Dee had received a life sentence without the eligibility for parole. He said that he regretted killing his wife and friend, but at the time he couldn't think because he was filled with rage.

Blinded by Rage

*We should take a minute to look at and think about our next step
Because things can get out of hand quickly and we will be in need of
some help.*

If we don't control our anger, but let our emotions run wild, *We
will end up doing something so stupid that it would even surprise a
child.*

*The fury and wrath of man worketh not the righteousness of God,
And if we continue to let it grow, we will be disciplined with His steel
and iron rod.*

*So keep your feelings in check and have the patience of a person
who is aged*

Because if we don't we will lose focus and be blinded by rage.
                    Poem by Antonio E walker

Way of Life

Wherefore my beloved bretheren, let every man be swift to hear, slow to speak, slow to wrath: For the wrath of man worketh not the righteousness of God.

James 1:20
(KJV)

Prayer

Lord Jesus,

I pray to You asking for Your help. There have been many times that my anger has gotten the best of me. Sometimes I have even

been so angry that it has turned into rage. I need You to help me control my temper Lord. I ask that You will please humble my heart when I am angry. Please Lord I can't do it without You.

In Your precious name I pray.

Amen!

Chapter Eighteen

Hard Headed

Whoever stubbornly refuses to accept criticism will suddenly be re-
covery.
Proverbs 29:1
(NLT)

Bread of Life

LORD, YOU ARE SEARCHING for honesty, you struck your people but they paid no attention. You crushed them, but they refused to be corrected. They are determined, with faces like stone; they have refusal to repent.

Jeremiah 5:3 (NLT)

Hard Head

Being stubborn and hard headed has caused e a lot of pain and suffering. It is one thing to be hurt by others, but it is a whole different story when you are beating our own head in with a stick. People have tried to help me all of my life; but being arrogant and filled with pride, I would do whatever I wanted. Sometimes, I knew that they were right; but didn't want to give them any *satisfaction, so I did the opposite of what they were telling me to do. By doing this, I have placed a lot of uncalled for obstacles n my life. If I would have just listened, I would have saved myself a lot of trouble and suffering.*

My mom used to always tell me to stop sucking on my bottom lip. It was just a habit I had picked up when I was five. A friend and I were playing on top of a garbage dumpster. Out of nowhere, she pushed me. I fell face-first busting my lip and knocking out two of my teeth. The next morning, my lip was swollen like a balloon. I started then sucking on my bottom lip and I never stopped, even though my mom told me that doing so would mess my teeth up. From my understanding, I could not see how sucking my lip would affect my teeth.

I ignored my mom, thinking that she was crazy. That is one of the biggest regrets I have in my life. I hate the way that my teeth stick out of my mouth. I look in the mirror and honestly feel that I am a handsome man besides my teeth. They make e look retarded and goofy. People don't take me seriously and always *think that I am smiling. All of my customers used to call me "Smiley".* Many women have told me that I am cute, but I have *heard many more say that I am ugly. I believe them both. I believe that everything about me is good looking except my teeth, which stick out of my mouth.*

If I had listened to my mom, I would have girls falling head over heels for me all through school. Because I didn't listen, I never *had a girlfriend while I was coming up. One of my goals in life has always been, and still s, to get my teeth fixed.*

I remember when Jamie Fox first started acting; he would play a woman by the name of Wanda. When someone saw her, they acted like they had seen a monster. That's how I *felt. After he got his teeth fixed he looked 100% better. Jamie Fox was a huge factor in my decision to get my teeth fixed.*

At one time, I did have braces. They made my confidence rise instantly, but I wound up going to jail. Because the county wouldn't pay for me to see an orthodontist, I had to have the *braces removed. It hurt me, but I told myself that I would get them fixed one day. I ended up putting gold in my mouth and settling for less.*

When I look back on my life, I think about not only that, but many decisions I have made. If I would have listened to warnings and constructive criticism, I would not be paying for it with unhappiness and wasted time from my life.

I tell myself that I am going to listen to everyone because I now realize that anyone can teach me something. There is a saying, "What's right, is right". This is so true, no matter where it *comes from.*

Someday I am, if I am blessed by God to do so, get my teeth fixed; but more importantly, I am going to stop being ignorant and hardheaded. When others are telling me the truth, I will listen to they say, whether I want to hear it or not. They also say that a hard head makes for a soft butt, and I am a living witness of that.

A Hard Head Makes a Soft Behind

HARDENING OUR HEARTS to criticism is an act of a fool,
The wise will listen carefully and use what they heard as a tool.
The truth will sometimes hurt and we won't like what we hear,
But that's just a part of life because we can't always control what goes into our ears.
Save ourselves the trouble and take heed to wise counsel, Accept what we are told, instead of showcasing our stubbornness on a mantel.
Being stuck in believing that everything we know is right
Is like believing in the darkness, but not believing in the light.
A person that knows everything is so hard and impossible to find,
But if we go by only what we know, we will quickly learn that a hard head makes a soft behind.
Poem by Antonio E Walker

Way of Life

The way of a fool is right in his own eyes: but he that harketh unto counsel is wise.

Proverbs 12:15
(KJV)

PRAYER

Chapter Nineteen

Obeying Our Parents

A wise son maketh a glad father: but a foolish son is a heaviness of
his mother
Proverbs 10:1
(KJV)

Bread of Life

Children obey your parents in the Lord: for this is right. Honour they father and mother; (which is the first commandment with promise) That it may be well with thee, and thou mayest live long on earth.
Ephesians 6:1-3
(KJV)

Problem Child

IS IT POSSIBLE TO GET worse at obeying our parents? Certainly! Our mothers and fathers couldn't do anything with us because we were hard headed. They tried to discipline and correct us, but usually, it was a waste of time. If you are a parent, then you can understand what I am talking about. You have probably tried everything possible to teach your children, but they continue doing the same old things and some begin doing worse.

I, like many other kids, was very disobedient. I was one of the worst growing up. I can't even count the number of spankings I *received and I stayed on punishment. I went to school only to get lunch and play at recess. I was smart, but not interested in doing or listening to anything. I did only the things that I wanted to do, and school work was not one of them. I brought home Fs in every class but PE. My mom would whoop me and take away my* privileges. After a while, I didn't care anymore. I caused so *much chaos at school I was tired when I got home anyway.*

Although I was bad then, I got much worse when I stepped into my first temporary foster care home and found out that I could do anything I wanted. The couple I lived with was older and was so warm and gentle. The atmosphere was so different from my home with my family.

We all sat at the dinner table together. In my whole life, my family had never done that except occasionally at restaurants.

The first time I had dinner at the foster home, while we would eat, some of the other kids started playing with their food and joking at the table. The couple asked them to stop. Some of the kids told them to shut up and the others ignored them. I was in shock at the way they talked to the foster parents. I found out quickly that the disrespect the kids showed the foster parents was a constant thing.

When I got placed in a permanent foster home, the parents were a little stricter and demanded a little more respect, but foster care is all about the kids. We could do or say anything we wanted without worrying about being spanked or cursed at. The only thing that the foster parents could do was take our privileges away. We always still got our allowance and got to go to all the same places the other kids went like the movies and bowling. We may not be able to watch TV or talk on the phone, but that wasn't a big deal to me or any other kid.

If a child caused too much trouble for the foster parents, they could call the kid's social worker and have them removed from the house. Some kids got to the point that no families would take them because the child was so hard to handle. Most of these kids wound up in group homes. They found out too late that it was better to obey the parents than to be in a group home.

Honor Thy Father and Mother

Everyone in this world is a child and must comply with what our parents tell us to do.

We are all created by God and He is our heavenly father, so listen to all He commands because He will guide us to what is true.

His words are to be obeyed because that is all that we have to help us left.

To not take heed and ignore Him is not only foolish but also leads to death.

A wise child makes their father happy, but a fool gives their mother a heavy heart

Walking and doing whatever pleases and satisfies their flesh and anything that is good they depart.

Don't be disrespectful and honor thy father and thy mother, Choosing anything different is living a life that's unfruitful and a life that's not worth the bother.

Poem by Antonio E Walker

Way of Life

Children, always obey your parents for this pleases the Lord.

Colossians 3:20
(NLT)

Prayer

My Savior,

I pray to you asking to repent and be forgiven for my sins. I have been stubborn in obeying your voice and statutes and

commandments. Please lead me Jesus, and soften my heart whenever I am Instructed or criticized by You, the Father, and others.

I love You and thank You for dying for my sins and correcting me.

Amen!

Chapter Twenty

Deceived by Looks

He that hateth with his lips, and lay up deceit within him.

Proverbs 26:24
(KJV)

Bread of life

He will be a master of deception and will become arrogant.

Daniel 8:25
(NLT)

Deceptive Lies

SINCE THE VERY FIRST woman and man, women have been some of the most deceptive beings on earth. Eve was deceived first by Satan and decided to deceive the man. I have been deceived by a few women myself mostly because I was too blind to see that they were only with me for my money.

At one time, I had been dating a girl, but I went to jail. After about a month, I called her to see what was going on. She said that she was pregnant by an older guy who was a big drug dealer. I wondered if the baby was really mine and she was just naming him the father because he had more money. I already knew she was a goldigger, and told myself that it didn't really matter. The older guy wound up going to prison. When it was almost tie for me to get out, all of a sudden she said that the baby was mine.

As it turned out, the baby was neither mine or the older guy's. *This just goes to show that women can be a mess sometimes.*

I have a friend who was also caught up in the same situation. He was dating a girl who got pregnant and told him that the child was his. My friend was so excited that he moved the girl into an apartment and took care of all the bills. He made her quit her job. He pampered her and made sure she was happy. All he ever talked about was her. He said that he had plans to marry her.

When it was time for the baby to be born, my friend recorded the whole birth. The baby was a little boy and was named after his father. When I saw the baby, I was surprised. My friend is as black as oil in the dark and the baby was light skinned.

After the birth, just like he said, my friend married the girl and moved her into a house. A couple of years went by. I still found it odd that the little boy did not favor my friend at all, but I didn't voice my opinion.

My friend and the girl began having problems and were separated for a while. The girl got pregnant during that time. My friend did not believe that the baby was his. They would argue, but she would always swear that she had never cheated on him. When she finally had the baby, he demanded a drug test for both children. Neither of the kids were his. And to make things worse, it finally came out that the children were his cousin's. My friend was *crushed.*

To this day, my friend does not trust any woman. And if you ask the woman, she blames it all on my friend. My friend didn't do *anything but love that woman and she did nothing but deceive him.*

Way of Life

Charm is deceptive, and beauty does not last; but a woman who fears the Lord will be greatly praised.
Proverbs 31:30
(NLT)

Prayer

Chapter Twenty-one

Being Deceptive

We know how unfair and oppressive we have been, carefully planning our deceitful lies.

Isaiah 59:13
(NLT)

Bread of Life

For they that are such serve not our Lord Jesus Christ, but their own belly; and by good words and fair speeches deceive the hearts of the simple.
Romans 16:18
(KJV)

Deceived by Looks

I only have one biological aunt, my mother's sister, but growing up I had too many to keep up with. All of y mom's female friends would tell my sisters and me to call them Aunty. I can't speak *for my sisters, but they always made me feel like a stud when they* were around. I have noticed that women don't remain friends for *too long. Maybe because of jealousy, envy, or lack of trust, but whatever the reason, they usually break their relationships pretty quickly. Men also end friendships, but for the most part, they remain friends longer than women.*

Most of y mom's friends would leave before I ever got attached to them. One of my mom's friends that was in and out of our lives was my aunt Marshall. She was one of my mother's childhood *friends and was always really nice to us. She had three children- three girls and one boy, who I still call my cousins to this day. Aunt Marshall and her kids would come over twice a month and spend the night at our house. I used to love it when they would come over because her oldest daughter and I would feel on each other and called ourselves boyfriend and girlfriend. My Aunt Marshall would chill with my mom.*

My Aunt Marshall had a boyfriend that used to beat her. I guess that one day she got tired of the abuse and pushed him. He fell down the stairs. When she could not get him to respond, she called the ambulance. The man was pronounced DOA. Aunt Marshall was arrested and charged with manslaughter. She received fifteen years and I never saw her again.

Another one of my mom's friends was named Darlene. She was *one of the most beautiful women I had ever seen. She had long hair, flawless skin, a pretty smile, and a gorgeous personality. She would come over and chill with my mom. I had a crush on her. I am not sure why her and my mom where so close, but they were very good friends. Darlene had lots of men of all different shapes, sizes and colors wanting o be her man; but for some* reason, she didn't have anyone that she was serious with.

Then out of nowhere, she started bring a guy named Steve around. You could tell by seeing them together that she really liked him. They dated for a while and eventually began falling in love. I liked very few men, but Steve was one of the ones I did. He was funny and treated my Aunt Darlene and my family very well.

One day, I came home from school to find my mom in tears. She told me that Darlene was dead and that Steve had killed her. I couldn't believe my ears. The story as my mother told it was that *Steve and Darlene had gone to a hotel and rented a room. Once in the room, they began to feel on one another. When they were both aroused, Darlene told Steve that she had something to tell him. She told him that her name was not Darlene. Her real name was Darrell.* Darrell was a man. I couldn't believe this and apparently Steve couldn't either because he began ripping off Darrell's clothes. When Darrell was naked, Steve saw his penis and went into a rage. He slit Darrell's throat and cut his penis *off. Steve then called the police and told them what happened.*

He was charged with murder.

Steve pled guilty to manslaughter and the judge gave him a ten year sentence. I used to feel a little sorry for Darrell. But, me being a man, I understood how Steve must have felt as well. I saw Steve as the victim of a very deceptive individual. If you would have seen Darrell, you would understand that he was a master of deception and filled with deceit.

Wolves in Disguise

Be careful anyone who deceives their neighbors through cunning and slick words,

Painting to others a pretty picture, but if we listen closely, we will notice what was said was being slurred.

There are even some who are so deceptive that they are masters of deceit,

They do and say things that are rare, remarkable, and unique.

Very dishonest looking for the first chance to double-cross, beguile, and betray,

Having no remorse for what they have done, only wanting to lead us astray.

So be on the lookout for wolves that are disguised

And for people who are always trying to pull the wool over our eyes.

Poem by Antonio E Walker

Way of Life

*But exhort one another daily, while it is called today; lest any of you
be hardened through the deceitfulness of sin.*
Hebrews 3:13
(KJV)

Prayer

Father,

Forgive me for being dishonest. I know that I have led others to believe things that I knew were untrue. I have lied and told others anything so that I could receive what I wanted. I am sorry for being deceptive and ask that you help me to change.

Amen!

Chapter Twenty-two

Hurtful Words

A gentle answer deflects anger, but harsh words make tempers flare.

Proverbs 15:1
(NLT)

Bread of Life

Let all bitterness, and wrath, and anger, and clamour, and evil speaking, be put away from you, with all malice.

Ephesians 4:31
(KJV)

The Power of Words

WHOEVER MADE UP THE saying "sticks and stones may break my bones, but words can never hurt me" must have either been a robot *or a very confident person who was really at peace with God. Words are very powerful. They can be used to heal and uplift or tear and destroy. Relationships have been restored and broken beyond re-pair through the power of words.*

People have said the most insignificant thing about me and I have been deeply offended and hurt. I am a person who has always held grudges. If someone said something that offended me, I resented that person. The words that hurt me the most were judgmental words. I hate for others to judge or voice their opinions when it comes to my character. I have always felt inferior to others, and when I hear nega-tive comments or remarks, I hated the one who said them.

Even truthful words hurt. I remember once I told a friend about my family situation at the time. I said that I had a reason for keeping my mom and sisters out of my life. His reply was that I was selfish. When he said that, it really hurt me. Although I did think about what he said, I became angry at him. I did not talk to him for months. I knew deep down that he was right, but refused to accept the fact.

Words can also start arguments, fights, and even lead to death. A person can be so filled with anger that they say anything just to hurt the other person's feelings. One day, I was arguing with a *guy from my hood. He said some things that made me want to kill him. It seemed that the angrier I got, the more he would say to add fuel to my anger. I got so mad at him that I drew my gun and pointed it in his face. While degrading me, he had been laughing like I was the joke of the day. Now that I had my pistol in his face, his whole attitude changed. He started apologizing and saying that he was only playing.*

Perhaps if there had not have been others around, I may have tak-en what he'd said as a joke and brushed it off, but everyone *there was laughing at me. The laughter of the others made my feelings of hurt and anger multiply. I still wanted to blow his head off for the things he had said, but I thought about the consequences that I would face, and lowered my gun. I walked* away and didn't look back.

From that day on, I was never the one chosen to be the target of jokes. I would still laugh when people joked on others and witnessed a lot of times that words lead to arguments, fights, and near death. It is easy to laugh when you are not the one being picked on and laughed at. When words are aimed at you, it doesn't seem to be funny any-more.

Title

When we get angry at someone, we should calm down and think about what is about to come out of our mouth.

If we let our emotions decide what is about to be said, our relationships can be damaged and we will be swinging at each other as if we are fighting in a championship bout.

The tongue is extremely powerful and a force that cannot be contained or controlled.

Our Lord Jesus Christ's help is needed or we will lose not only our *lives but also our souls.*

Watch your words carefully and pot God first in your life each and every day,

And when we speak we should always be certain that we say what we mean and we mean what we say.

Poem by Antonio E Walker

Way of Life

Kind words are like honey – sweet to the soul and healthy for the body.

Proverbs 16:24
(NLT)

Chapter Twenty-three

Slandering Others

Thou shalt not bear false witness against thy neighbor
Exodus 20:16

$\left(\mathrm{K}^{JV)}\right.$

Bread of Life

You love to destroy others with your words, you liar!
Psalm 52:4
(NLT)

Slanderous Lies

I KNOW THAT MANY PEOPLE, including me, hate being lied to or lied about! People have very vivid imaginations. They can come up with stories and fibs that are as big as a whale. Some of the most popular pastimes like sports, video games, movies, etc. came to exist because someone thought, imagined, and put their idea into action.

I have been the victim of many slanderous lies that really hurt me. People have told others that I used to eat out of trash cans, that I was snitching, and that I had AIDS, to name just a few. When I heard of these lies, it hurt my pride more than my feelings. I used to wonder why people would make up things about me,

knowing that what they said was not true. I would try to track down the person who had lied, but always came to a dead end.

One of the most hurtful lies ever told about me was revealed when my mother and I were in an argument. I was saying that I didn't want anything to do with her. She responded, saying that she didn't care because all that I wanted to do *was snort powder anyway. When she* said that, I exploded. I knew that she had probably heard someone else say that about me; and by the way she said it, I knew that she believed the lie. I called her every name that I could think of and I have not seen her since. I have forgiven her and hope that she will forgive me for the things I said.

People will say anything to bring you down. My roommates in prison slander other prisoners. At one time, my roommate owned a phone and other guys would pay him to use it. If one of the guys' girlfriends would call back, my roommate would go and get the person. If, for whatever reason, a guy who had used the phone left the dorm, my roommate would call his girl. He would tell them that her boyfriend had been put in the hole or moved and act like he was concerned for the guy. He would take messages back and forth between the two until he and the girl became friends. Once he had won her *trust, he would tell the girl that her boyfriend was having sex with other men.*

I would sit on my bunk and listen to my roommate. I said nothing. Knew that he thought that he would never get caught in his lies or that, if he did, he had homeboys to warn him or protect him. He did get caught once. One of the girls he'd lied to didn't *believe him and told her boyfriend. Luckily, when the guy got out* of the hole, he was moved to a different dorm; but that didn't stop *him from sending death threats to my roommate. Then one day, while my roommate was in the gym playing basketball, out of nowhere the guy ran onto the court and stabbed my roommate twelve times. I felt sorry for my roommate, but I also knew that he had brought it upon himself by spreading slanderous lies about other people.*

Slanderous Words

HE THAT REFRAINETH his lips is a very intelligent and wise man, But he that uses words that are untruthful is someone who doesn't care that their death will be n high demand.

A person who loves to falsely accuse others will not have and long life to live,

He will be badly beaten for his lies and sometimes even killed.

Spreading rumors is like entering a dark cave that has no source of light,

Blindly walking until being tripped up or awakened by an angry bear that will want to fight.

Those who speak kindly and honestly about others will be cherished and admired,

To prevent destroying others with slanderous words is quite simple, just stop being a liar.

Poem by Antonio E Walker

Way of Life

He that hideth hatred with lying lips, and he that uttereth a slander is a fool. In the multitude of words there wanteth not sin: but he that refraneth his lips is wise.

Proverbs 10:18-19

(KJV)

Prayer

My Lord Jesus,
I call upon You for mercy. Asking that You forgive me and put it on the hearts of others to forgive me for the gossip and lies that I have spread that I knew weren't true. I will go from this day forth speaking only about the positive things and only the truth.
Amen!

Chapter Twenty-four

Foolish Choices

Better is a poor and wise child than s an old and foolish king, who will no more be admonished.

Ecclesiastes 4:13
(KJV)

Bread of Life

He made a pit and digged it, and is fallen into the ditch which he has made.

Psalm 7:15
(KJV)

A Costly Decision

ONE OF MY FAVORITE pastimes s fishing. There is just something about being out on the river with a couple of friends relaxing in the peaceful presence of nature. Me and a couple of buddies used to go out on the Chattahoochee River on Sundays to fish. We would have to sneak and be careful that the game warden wouldn't catch us because we had no fishing license.

We also had to be aware of the dam. At any given time, the dam could be opened and we would have to hurry off of the river as the water quickly rose. A siren would sound to let everyone know that the dam was being opened. When the damn opened, the currents in the river could be as powerful as ocean waves. The only way that a person has a chance of making it across is in a speedboat.

My friends and I were caught by the game warden, but got off with a warning. We were fortunate enough to have never had the dam open up on us. But not everyone was that blessed.

In the river, there are big rocks that are visible when the damn is closed. You could find catfish, crappies, and small bass there. These rocks make a great fishing spots. But if the damn ever opened, the area would flood quickly and the rocks would be covered.

There were two men who went down to the river to fish. They set up on one of the big rocks in the middle of the river. They had food, bait, and alcohol. After a couple of hours of fishing, eating, and drinking, the guys had become highly intoxicated. The siren sounded to alert people that the damn was about to open. The river started to rise and before they knew what was happening, the water started covering the rock they were on. Finally, one of the guys realized what was happening and told the other. Luckily for them, after a couple of minutes, the dam closed. The top of the rock that they were on was still above water, but the rocks they had jumped across to get to the middle of the river had disappeared and they were trapped.

Eventually, one of the guys was panicking and began to get hysterical. It was getting dark, and he was afraid that the damn would open again and wash them away. He told his friend that he was going to swim across and get some help. The other guy told him not to try to swim in the water because the currents were too strong to swim, but his friend jumped in anyway.

After a minute or so, the guy in the water realized that his friend was right and tried to turn back. He screamed for his friend to help him. His friend wanted to help him with all his heart, but there was nothing he could do but watch his friend sink and disappear. The guy who remained on the rock was crushed. At about 8:30 the next morning, the game warden found the man and rescued him. The police found the body of his friend. If only the man had chosen to be patient like his friend, he would still have been alive. He made a wrong decision and foolishly died because of it.

The Choice is Ours

No one can make us do or feel that we don't want to do or feel. *God gave us this life to live out in love and the gift of free will.*

We are not able to blame anyone for the decisions that we make, We all have the ability to comprehend and decide what is the best step we should take.

The prudent sees the danger ahead and avoids it at all cost, But a fool will continue to walk as if he doesn't see it and pretend that he is lost.

When the consequences come and they are harsh and severe, He will have to suffer in them because the choice was always his.

Poem by Antonio E Walker

Way of Life

*A prudent person foresees danger and takes precautions.
The simpleton goes blindly on and suffers consequences.*

(NLT)

Prayer

Chapter Twenty-five

Cross Roads

There is a path before each person that seems right but it ends n death.
Proverbs 14:12
(NLT)

Bread of Life

Shew me thy ways, Oh Lord; Teach me thy paths.

Psalm 25:4
(KJV)

Hitting the Highway

DRIVING DOWN I-85 IS dangerous when it is raining. The highway becomes very slick. One mistake could cause a multiple vehicle wreck. It is even more risky for two black men who are trafficking cocaine.

If a drug dealer travels out of town to buy cocaine, you could make a lot more money. If a kilo went for $21,000 in Columbus, you could travel to Atlanta and purchase it for $18,000. The only catch is the risk involved in bringing it back. State troopers patrol the highways looking for drug traffickers who most law enforcement officers assume to be either Latino or African American. I made plenty of runs on I-85, but lucky for me, I never even got pulled over. I know a lot of people who were not so fortunate.

I know a guy who used to run dope from Miami to Columbus. He would use mules who were likely to run under the radar without being suspicious. Women, especially white women, are the best mules.

I met this guy through a female friend of mine that would make trips for him. She would take her kids with her, be gone for two days, and return without any problem. She would always throw a party when she got back to town. Her name was Red. She was a thick, high-yellow, and curvy woman with a beautiful face and personality. I had a crush on her, but she was in love with her children's father. That didn't stop me from trying though. *One morning, Red was supposed to make her run, but her little girl was sick. When she called to tell the guy her dilemma, he got really upset. She called me and asked me if I wanted to make $10,000.* I wasn't sure that I wanted to take the risk. My life wasn't all that, but it was a lot better than spending 15 to 20 *years in a federal penitentiary.*

Red eventually found a girl who agreed to make the trip. The girl apparently made it to Miami and picked up the drugs. On her way back, the police where at one of the turnpikes with K-9s. When the dogs approached the girl's car, they went crazy. *The police searched her vehicle. What they discovered made the news. They found 32 kilos of cocaine and 50 lbs of marijuana. They haled the girl off to jail and charged her with drug trafficking. She received 180 months in the Federal Penn. I thank God that he allowed me to think and make the right choice. If I had made the wrong choice, it would have cost me many years of my life.*

The Proper Way

Smart people choose the right paths but morons choose the wrong. Fools will have a very wicked and short life, while the wise will live prosperous and long.

Idiots think the road s acceptable and foolishly travel on, When out of nowhere comes death and destruction, their souls and minds are gone.

Wisdom and knowledge comes from the Lord with understanding in his hand.

And with them He leads the sane along to carry out his plans.

The righteous do it willingly and receive insight every day.

They choose what is agreeable and are shown the proper way.

Poem by Antonio E Walker

Way of Life

A wise person chooses the right road; a fool takes the wrong one.
Ecclesiastes 10:2
(NLT)

Prayer

Lord Jesus,

I come to You humbly asking to be led. I have been making a lot of bad choices and decisions. I'm not wise in my decision making and I need You Lord. Please let me be able to take heed in the criticism that others give me. Soften my heart Lord to do what is wise, even when I don't want to. Amen!

Chapter Twenty-six

Jesus Loves Us

As the Father hath loved me, so I have loved you: continue ye in my love. If ye keep my commandments, ye shall abide n my love; even as I have kept my Fathers commandments, and abide in his love.

John 15:9-10

(KJV)

Bread of Life

He that hath my commandments, and keepeth them, he it is that loveth me; and he that will loveth me shall be loved of my Father. And I will love him, and will manifest myself to him.

John 14:21

(KJV)

Putting Things Before Christ

I got sent to a halfway house after serving 42 months of my prison sentence. I prayed to Jesus, asking Him to allow me the opportunity to be accepted and I was. When I first got there, I told myself that I was not going to do anything that might get me sent back to prison.

The first 14 days were fairly easy. I stayed drug-free and out of trouble. I read my Bible and wrote these books. Then I realized how the house was run. If a resident got caught smoking, drinking, or doing drugs; they just got fined. I watched others doing whatever they wanted, and getting away with it.

I had been addicted to marijuana since I was a teen. After a couple weeks at the halfway house, I tricked myself into believing that I could do as everyone else was doing. I started smoking again. I stopped praying and reading the Bible. I stopped writing and abandoned my goals. Al I wanted to do was smoke weed, eat, talk on the phone to girls, and plan what I was going to do with the money I would be saving. I decided that I was going to buy cocaine to cook and sell. That lasted exactly 15 more days.

Four days before I was allowed to go out and look for a job, I was relaxing and smoking a joint. I didn't think I had a care in the world.

A corrections officer that worked at the halfway house caught me smoking. He took me to the hole and wrote a disciplinary report on me. I sat in the hole and was confident that I would be given another chance. I prayed to Jesus every day, asking Him to forgive me, promising that if He gave me another chance I would do right. I stayed in the hole for 21 days and then I was shipped back to prison.

On the bus back to the prison, I was mad at Jesus and hurt that He had not given me another chance at the halfway house. I had no money, no clothes, and no shoes. I was going back to prison with nothing. I felt betrayed and forsaken.

As soon as these thoughts came into my mind, Jesus spoke to me as clear as He ever has. He told me that I was the one who had betrayed Him. When I was in prison, I had prayed and asked Him to bless me. As soon as he did, I turned my back on Him. I chose marijuana and doing my own will over writing these books and doing God's will. I put other things before Him and started *loving them, forgetting who had been there for me my entire life. Jesus showed me that just as He can give out of love, He can also take away out of love. He had allowed me to go back to prison to get my attention, and He accomplished it.*

Jesus Loves Us

Can anything in this world separate us from the love of Christ, He is our leader who leads by example and showed us compassion by giving up his life.

A loving Savior who rescues us from our sins,

He openly fights our battles and always comes up with a win.

God is in Him, and He is in us,

So give up all your doubts and in Him put your trust.

With Him we have overcome satan and his devices of death,

He tried to trick us right into hell, but Jesus made us go left.

He loves us and will always give us what is needed,

Therefore we will always be provided for, even f it's a drought *season.*

Poem by Antonio E Walker

Way of Life

Can anything ever separate us from Christ's love? Does it mean *he no longer loves us if we have trouble or calamity, or are persecuted, or hungry, or destitute, or in danger, or threatened with death?* (As the Scriptures say, "For your sake we are killed *every day; we are being slaughtered like sheep.) No, despite all these things, overwhelming victory is ours through Christ, who loved us.*
Romans 8:35-37
(NLT)

Feelings of Weakness

One afternoon, while at basketball tryouts, I discovered a trait that would be a hindrance on my desires, dreams and goals for most of my life. It's a trait that everyone has obtained in their life at some point. It's a trait in which also gives birth to other ungodly traits such as fear, jealousy, and doubt. This trait gives us feelings of weakness in our abilities. When I was a young teen, I remember growing up playing basketball on the playgrounds and school yards. I had a nice jump shot or, as some may call it, a nice stroke. I could dribble pretty well and was a pretty decent defender. So when the time came to try out for my middle school basketball team, I naturally thought I was guaranteed to make the team. When the tryouts began I couldn't buy a basket or even make a simple layup. It seemed to me that everyone else was making all of their shots. I recall becoming very discouraged and started feeling weaker than the other guys that were trying out. Soon the self pity crept in and I asked myself why I even was wasting my time when the other guys looked like super stars compared to my intangible basketball skills. I made a promise not to embarrass myself anymore and I left the tryouts crying and never returned. This is just one situation in my life in which I have faced feelings of weakness in myself and my abilities. In this book you will find out how I overcame this false trait and how you can also overcome misleading feelings, false ideas, and false traits that you may believe about yourself. You will also learn that nothing is impossible for us because

We can do all things through Christ which strengthens us. Philippians 4:13(KJV)

Believing in Christ

TRUST AND BELIEVE IN Christ. He believed in and loved you so much that He gave his life so that you have the opportunity to live with Him and His Father in Heaven forever. All you have to do is accept, trust, and believe Him in your heart.

Bread of Life

He tells what he has seen and heard, but how few believe what he tells them! Those who believe him
discover that God is true. For he is sent by God. He speaks God's words, for God's Spirit is upon him
without measure or limit. The Father loves his Son, and he has given him authority over everything. 36 And all who believe in God's Son have eternal life.
Those who don't obey the Son will never experience eternal life, but the wrath of God remains upon them.
John 3:32-36
(NLT)

Having No Belief

During my elementary years, my teachers used to always tell me that I was very smart for my age. Their words encouraged me and made me feel special. Even so, I hated going to school. My classmates used to call me "buck tooth", "beaver", "walrus", and many other hurtful names. I have had a big overbite for as long as I can remember so, naturally, the nickname "Buck" stuck.

I felt violated and became offensive even if others thought they were only kidding and making jokes. I started not only having hateful feelings towards my peers, but also towards myself. I felt discouraged and thought of myself as an ugly and deformed monster. I did not know then that these hurtful names would cause me to have a low self-esteem and lead me to feel very uncomfortable around people. I became timid and still have what most call "shyness". I believe the correct word for it is low self-esteem.

I used to envy other guys who I saw as better looking than me. When I saw them with their girlfriends I would wish that I was them; or that I at least had a girlfriend of my own. I didn't end up getting my first girlfriend until later in my life at the age of sixteen.

I did not believe in myself, my capabilities, or my talents. I had no future goals and soon began fighting, stealing and getting in all kinds of trouble in school. My grades never were that good in the first place. Before long, I was failing and making all F's every year. I ended up giving up on school and everything important. I dropped out of school in the ninth grade.

I felt like a failure in everything I tried to accomplish. I was very stubborn, bitter, hard-headed. I didn't want anyone telling me what to do, especially when to me they weren't helping my life in anyway. I decided to run away from the foster home i was living.

When I hit the streets and started living on my own, others success and happiness often upset and depressed me. I became angry at the world and was jealous of anyone who appeared to be successful. So, I started selling drugs. I was good at it and quickly made lots of money. This success gave me hope that I could be somebody. I told myself that I was going to be very successful one day.

To me, success meant having beautiful women, cars, clothes, and lots of money. Even though I was raised in the church and taught to trust and believe in God and His Son Jesus Christ, I ended up believing in money instead. I adopted the false belief that only way I would ever become somebody important was by having money. I thought money would lead me to success and put all my trust into making it by any means necessary. I had no trust in God and had very little faith and belief in his son Jesus Christ.

Regain Control

We all have faced obstacles and we all have done things that took our eyes off of God, and it ended up leading us astray.

But if you want to be able to accomplish anything in your life, you must Pray to Jesus Christ and ask Him for direction because He will show you the only and the right way.

It will sometimes become very, very difficult to put aside are own desires and selfish intentions,

but if you decide to give your troubles and worries to the Lord, he will anoint and prosper all of your greatest ambitions.

So flee from anything that takes your eyes off of

God and makes you do things that you know you should not do

Because you will become a slave to anything that you put before Him and it will eventually take control over you.

Regain control!

Poem by Antonio E. Walker

Way of Life

WHOEVER BELIEVES THAT Jesus is the Christ is born of
God, and everyone who loves Him who begot also loves him who
is begotten of Him. By this we know that
we love the children of God, when we love God and keep His commandments."

1 John 5:1-2
(NKJV)

WHO IS HE WHO OVERCOMES the world, but he who believes
that Jesus is the Son of God! 1 John 5:5

1 John 5:5
(NKJV)

Prayer

Lord Jesus,

I pray to You seeking mercy, love, and guidance.

Without You I wouldn't be here. I know and believe that You died for me and my sins. I ask that You please forgive me for not always believing and losing faith at times. Thank You so much for kindness and patience and for always believing in me even though I sometimes fall weak in the flesh. I know, trust, and believe You will lead into a better life in this world, and also into heaven. In Your name I pray.

Amen!

Trusting In God

Trust in the Lord of Hosts. There is nothing in the heavens above or here on earth that He doesn't control. You can trust Him with your life because He will never ever lead us wrong.

Bread of Life

Trust in the LORD with all your heart; do not depend on your own
understanding.
Proverbs 3:5
(NLT)

I Didn't Trust Anyone

When I was growing up, life was a constant struggle most of the time for me and my family. I have three sisters. My mom was, for the majority of the time, a single parent although my youngest sister's father, Smoky, was in and out of our lives. Smoky was the only father figure I had ever known. Most of the time when he was home, he and my mom would fight and argue. Then he would leave. During Smokey's absences, my mom would tell me that I was the man of the house and that it was my responsibility to protect her and my sisters. I loved and cherished that role because it made me feel like an important and strong man.

Each time Smoky came back, I hated it with a passion. He would usually return high on drugs or drunk on alcohol. He would either fell asleep or start beating my mom up in front of me and my sisters. I used to try and help my mom fight him but he was too big and strong for me. So I would run to the nearest pay phone and call the police. When the police arrived, sometimes my mom would press charges and they locked him up. But many times my mom decided not to press charges against him. I never understood why she would keep taking him back after he constantly beat on her. The more she let him get away with beating her the more I started doubting everything she taught me.

As I grew older, I lost complete trust in her, God, and myself. I came to falsely believe that life was all about being lucky or unlucky. It seemed to me that I was just an unlucky kid whose mom was incompetent and whose family happened to be very poor. I believe the world was against me. I did not trust in God, in His will, His plan for my life, or in His power and ability to change my life. I did not put my trust in anything or anyone.

Trusting in God

Thank You Almighty Father for being a just and kind
Creator,
A God who is loving towards all followers and believers and even towards those who accept Your word later.

Truthful always to the words that You state, You will always be by our side,

Wanting us to have faith in You- never worrying about trouble or looking for a place to hide.

All we have to do is trust in You and truly believe,

Because we are born into Your love and grace, and that's where we will stay until it is time for us to leave.

Thank You Father for loving us even when we couldn't love our self,

Thank You for providing for us when we were hungry and looking in the wrong places for wealth.

Praise You Lord for being there for us when situations got hard and a little rough,

For it is in You, and only You, that I give my heart, soul ,and, mind
And in You only do I put my trust.
Poem by Antonio E. Walker

Way of Life

And we have a priceless inheritance—an inheritance that is kept in
heaven for you, pure and undefiled,

BEYOND THE REACH OF change and decay. [5] And through
your faith, God is protecting you by his power until you receive this
salvation, which is ready to be revealed on the last day for all to see.

1 Peter 1:4-5
(NLT)

Prayer

Heavenly Father,

I put my trust in You for everything and I cherish Your wise and wonderful guidance. I trust in Your mercy and understanding. Thank You for always taking care of me. I know that Your love is what wakes me up in the morning. My life is Yours to use any way You choose and I have no worries because You have always protected me from danger. Please forgive me for all my sins and I promise to trust You with my mind, heart, and soul. In Jesus name I pray.

Amen!

Born Into Sin

We all are born into sin, but we don't have to stay in Sin. If you want to be released from sin, you have to accept Jesus Christ as your Lord and Savior with your mouth and your heart and ask Him for forgiveness of your sins and you will be forgiven.

Bread of Life

For I was born a sinner – yes, from the moment my mother conceived me,

But you desire honesty from the heart, so you can teach me to be wise in my inmost being.

Purify me from my sins, and I will be clean; wash me, and I will be whiter than snow.

Psalms 51:5-7

(NLT)

Sinning at an Early Age

I started stealing at the age of six. At the time, my mom was struggling to take care of me and my sisters. The first of every month was like Thanksgiving; but toward the end of the month, it became extremely hard for us. I remember sometimes we didn't have anything other than buttered rice, or popcorn to eat. Even though I love popcorn or any kind of corn, anything you are eating for breakfast, lunch, and dinner will lose its allure very quickly.

The first thing I stole was a twenty dollar bill from my Uncle Junior's wallet. My family and I were living with him at the time. I remember sneaking into his room while he was asleep one night. He always kept his wallet on his nightstand next to his bed. I crept up and opened up the wallet. I don't know if he had just gotten paid or what, but he was banked up. I remember convincing myself that if I just took one of the bills he would never know. So I slid a bill out, closed the wallet, placed it exactly how I had found it, and took off out of the room. When I looked at the bill and saw that it was a twenty, I felt like the richest kid in the world. I had never been given anything more than a dollar. I ended up spending all of the money on snacks and candy.

I was young, but I knew it was wrong to steal from others, but I didn't care. All I could think about was all of the things I was going to buy. At the time, I didn't know that I was going to keep on stealing until I would eventually become addicted to doing it. I was living in a very sinful world and I was sinning at a very early age.

Born into Sin

The Holy Spirit that's inside of me
Says to do the right thing,
But my urge tells me to forget
About what's being said,
And to carry out my own wicked scheme.
I want to do right and I try hard to be a good being, But I keep
backsliding doing any and everything.
Sinful in my ways
And sometimes even in my dreams, Hurting people along the way
just to get what I need.
Feeling remorseful, regretful,
And also low and ashamed,
But I have been doing wrong for so long, Since the first day that I was
named.
I tell myself over and over that I will change
And never do it again, But it gets hard along the way at times,
Being that I was born into a world full of sin.
Poem by Antonio E. Walker

Way of Life

IF WE SAY THAT WE HAVE no sin, we deceive ourselves, and the truth is not in us. If we confess, He is
 faithful and just to forgive us our sins and to cleanse us from all unrighteousness. If we say that we have not sinned, we make him a liar and his word is not in us.
 1 John 1:8-10 (NKJV)

Chapter Four

Having Hope in God

When you ask God for something, you must hope, trust, and belief that He will give it to you. And you will receive it, but you must also have patience.

Bread of Life

So I pray that God, Who gives you hope, will keep you
Happy and full of peace as you believe in Him. May you overflow
with hope through the Power of the Holy Spirit.
Romans15:13
(NLT)

Losing Hope

When I turned 11 in 1991, my life, which was already drastic, got even worse. My mom had always taught my sisters and me to be respectable towards adults, to care for and share with each other, and especially not to act out in public or in front of her company. Disobedience of any of these rules was like asking for a death wish.

I loved my mom dearly. The only real happiness I recall having as a child was during the times that we were together (minus the times my sister's dad was present). My mom always would make up adventurous stories to tell us and take us to the movies or out to eat when money permitted- usually around the first of the month.

I enjoyed playing house with my sisters and going into the woods and pretending that we were out hunting wild animals. These were happy and peaceful times for me, when it was just us. I still stole and acted up sometimes, but not that much.

One day during that time, I recall looking into the bathroom and finding a soda can with little burn holes poked in it. I picked it up and smelled it. It smelled like burnt hair and gasoline. I was bright for my age and knew something had been smoked on it, but I did not know what or by whom until I saw my mom going in and out of the bathroom.

I was in D.A.R.E (Drug Abuse Resistance Education) classes at school and the police used to teach my classmates and me all about the dangers of drug use. They taught us that drugs make us dumber, slower, can influence us to do things that we would not usually do, and could even kill us. Seeing my mom going in and out of the bathroom and staying for long periods made me wonder what drug she was smoking. I already knew that she smoked marijuana in little white rolling papers, and I knew that whatever she was smoking now was different.

I used to pray that my mom would leave my youngest sisters father alone. I hoped that she would meet a man that could help change my family's lives for the better. When I found out that she was smoking and hooked on crack cocaine, I started losing Hope that any of these things would ever happen.

Hope and Believe

Hope for a long life with guidance from the Lord,

Believe in His son Jesus Christ, in His power, and in His Word as your sword.

Hope for His mercy and keeping you protected from harm, know that God is your everything, your shelter in the storm.

Hope for a change inside that leads you to doing what is right, believe and know for sure that He will never let you out of His sight.

Hope for God's strength when circumstances seem to be too much, believe and He will carry you for He is an unbreakable crutch.

Hope for sunshine even if the forecast predicts dark skies, believe that God can do anything because there

is nothing comparable to Him, and nothing exists that is as powerful and wise.

Poem by Antonio E. Walker

Way of Life

Blessed is the man who trusts in the Lord.
AND WHOSE HOPE IS THE Lord.
Jeremiah 17:7
(NKJV)

Prayer

Heavenly Father, K

I will put my hope and belief in You. Praise Your Holy name for always being loving, gentle, and kind to me. I know times might seem hard for me right now, but I know they could be a lot worse. Thank You Father. All You have ever shown me is love. I love You and hope to live with You forever in this life and in heaven. Amen!

Never Separated From Christ

Jesus is our Savior, Friend, Brother, and Lord. He is always with us in everything and will never forsake us or our hope. In times of distress you can always depend and ~~count~~ on His glorious presence.

Bread of Life

Can anything ever separate us from Christ's love?

Does it mean he no longer loves us if we have trouble or calamity, or are persecuted, or are hungry, or cold or in danger or threatened with death? (Even the

scriptures say, for your sake we are killed every day; we are being slaughtered like sheep") No despite all these things, Overwhelming victory is ours through

Christ, who has loved us. And I am convinced that nothing can ever separate us from his love. Death

can't, and life can't. The angels can't, and demons can't. Our fears about today, our worries about

tomorrow. And even the powers of hell can't keep

God's love away. Whether we are above the sky, or the deepest oceans, nothing in all creation will be able to separate us from the love of God that is revealed in Christ Jesus our Lord.

Romans 8:35-38

(NLT)

Growing Separate from My Mother

Whoever made up the name "controlled substance" hit it right on the nail. My mom was slowly distancing herself from my sisters and me more and more every day. I don't know if she knew it or not, but we all could tell that her focus was on something other than us. Even though my family had it hard coming up, one thing that had stayed consistent was my mom showing us plenty of love, discipline, and attention. That began to change. Whatever was in the bathroom was now more important to her than us and it controlled her time.

She started having strange men and women come around who smelled horrible. Whenever her company came over she made my sisters and me go outside and told us to go play over our friends' homes. We already struggled to make it out of the month with something to eat. Now that she was using crack it was becoming more difficult and unbearable for my sisters and me. We stopped going to the movies and out to eat. She started telling us that she didn't have any extra money to give us.

I began to even appreciate going to school. This was not because I wanted to learn, but because I knew I would have two guaranteed meals that day- breakfast and lunch. Each day the issues grew worse. Eventually my mom hardly even came out of her room, and if she did it was only for a few moments to open the door for her friends.

I didn't learn until late one night when I was awakened by flash lights and police officers that I was living in a crack house. The police took my sisters and me to my grandmother's house and took my mom and her friends to jail. At that time, I had never been away from my mom in my twelve years of living. Now we would be separated for a little over a year.

Jesus Is With You

Jesus is with you and you are forever in His care,
Whether your situation is calm or in times that you must be aware.
Jesus is your strength, your foundation, and also your shield,
He is the farmer that picks the worries and rocks from our fields.

We are never separate from His love and kindness, In times when you aren't able to see, He is your lamp of strong guidance.

We are also never separate from His power, glory, and will.

Jesus is in you and if evil is there, by his authority it will be removed and killed.

So keep faith, for in your life He has always kept in touch, Jesus has been with you and never for a second will He ever leave us.

Poem by Antonio E. Walker

Way of Life

Teaching them to observe all things that I have commanded you; and logic given you.

And be sure of this: I am with you always, even to the end of the age!

Matthew 28:20
(NKJV)

Prayer

Lord Jesus Christ,

Thank You for loving me so much. You died for my sins and I know You have never left my side, even though sometimes my behavior says different. Please forgive me Lord for my many sins and falling short of Your example. I will do better knowing that I will never be separated from your love and presence. In Your precious name I pray.

Amen!

Chapter Six

We Have a Friend in Jesus

Jesus is our friend to the end. He hears all our prayers and knows our desires. You receive blessings you didn't ask for everyday. That is Jesus blessing you out of His love. He knows the dreams of everyone on earth and, if they line up with the will of God, they will become a reality. That is what a true friend is for - to help us succeed. And believe me, Christ is your best friend.

Bread of Life

A MAN WHO HAS FRIENDS must himself be friendly, but there is a friend who sticks closer than a brother.

Proverbs 18:24
(NLT)

CHAPTER 6 TEST

CHAPTER 6 POEM

Way of Life

I command you to love each other in the same way that I have loved
you.
And here is how to measure it.
The greatest love is shown when people lay down their lives for their
friends.
You are my friends if you follow my commands.
John 15:12-14
NO BOOK

~~CHAPTER 6 PRAYER~~

Chapter Seven

Our Destructive Ways

We have to be extremely careful about how we live our lives. Sometimes living the wrong way can make us feel happy, but if we aren't living and obeying God's word, we are headed for destruction.

BREAD OF LIFE

Unfailing love and faithfulness cover sin; evil is avoided by fear of the Lord. When the ways of people please the Lord, He makes even their enemies live at peace with them.

Proverbs 16:6-7

(NLT)

I Thought I Was Grown

Almost every teenager comes to a stage in their life when they believe they are grown. They think that no one can tell them anything. I came to this stage when I turned 14. My sisters and I were living back with my mom in a slum-infested neighborhood known for having a sky-high crime rate. My mom had been out of jail for about six months. She had started smoking crack again. She and I argued and clashed a lot. I hardly ever listened to what she told me. Deep inside I felt she couldn't tell me anything because she was strung out on cocaine.

To get away from her, I started hanging in the streets with drug dealers, staying in their company instead of that of my family. I still went to school, but only to eat, after which I would slip back out into the streets. Eventually, I started selling drugs myself and breaking into cars. I always had one to two hundred dollars on me. I felt like a millionaire. I was in the streets hustling at an early age. I loved making my own money because my mom couldn't say that she fed or did anything for me.

Meanwhile, my mom was getting worse and more strung out on crack each day. Most times when I returned home, crack heads would be everywhere. Every time I saw them I would become very angry and storm into my room, change clothes, and then head right back to the streets. One day when I returned, the police were there once again. Once again, my mom's crack house had been busted.

My mom for told the police to take my sisters and me to her mother's house. When they took us there, my grandmother told them she couldn't take care of us anymore because we didn't mind her or behave. So, we were taken to our uncle's house and he agreed to take care of us.

I didn't want to stay with my uncle because he was strict and had a lot of rules. So, I ran away that night and started staying at some of my friends' homes, empty houses, or in the streets. I stole, broke into cars, sold drugs and ate whatever I pleased. I gave up on going to school altogether. I did whatever I wanted to do and thought that I was a grown man because I was hustling. I thought I was doing a great job of taking care of myself.

Our Destructive Ways

Some days will fly by quick, but some are real slow, Money will pile thick and money will get low.

Greed can set in and we'll do almost anything,
Whether it is good or bad, Just to see a diamond's bling.
Some men like their ladies big and some like them small,
But if they have lust within their hearts, They will sleep with them all.

Some of our ways can direct us towards Hell, Because our sinful nature doesn't follow God, Nor did the Angel that fell.

Change your life and always listen to instructions, Because if we are living the wrong way, We are headed for destruction.

It's really quite simple-

All you have to do is listen to the voice of God within your heart that is telling us to stop all the wickedness and evilness

And go to His Son Christ Jesus for forgiveness. So pray and say you're sorry, then repent from your wicked days,

And live a life to see heaven
And turn from your destructive ways.

POEM BY ANTONIO E. Walker

Way of Life

You shall walk in all the ways which the Lord your God has commanded you, that you may live and that it may be well with you. And that you may prolong your days in the land which you shall possess.

Deuteronomy 5:35
(NKJV)

Prayer

Lord Jesus,

I pray to You asking for Your mercy and forgiveness for all of my sins. Please forgive me for my destructive ways, I'm sorry Lord and repent from these ways. I know I haven't been living right, but from this day forth i will strive to live in a way that is pleasing to God. Thank You for Your patience with me and I will not let your death for me go in vain. Instead I will change my ways and live how I am supposed to. In your name, Lord Jesus, I pray.

Amen!

Chapter Eight
Help From Above

EVERYONE HAS FALLEN off the correct path. But the Lord loved us so much that He gave His only son Jesus Christ to die for us. But Jesus is risen and we can come to Him with repentance in our hearts and He will help us back onto the right road.

Bread of Life

Fear not, for I am with you; be not dismayed, fore I am your God.
I will strengthen you, yes, I will help you.
Isaiah 41:10
(KJV)

X DC he

Help From Above

I RAN THE STREETS, sold drugs, and took care of myself for about 5 months. My mom had received another year of jail time and I was waiting on her to get out. I planned on moving back in with her and my sisters when she got out. I was hoping that she would stay off of drugs this time when she was released.

I was making around 50.00 a day and told myself that I was going to have enough money saved to help my family and buy them all the things that they had always wanted. One day, while I was standing on the corner selling crack, the police rode up and jumped out of their cars. I took off running but ended up being caught and searched, but not before I had threw the drugs I had on me.

Seeing that I was a young teen, they asked me where I stayed at. When I told them I lived on my own, they took me to the Department of Family and Children Services (DFACS). They spoke with a caseworker who introduced herself to me and told me that she was going to find me a good home with nice parents. She started calling foster parents and asked them if they would accept me in their home. Many of them turned her down, but after a while, she finally found me a new home.

She drove me to a nice 4 bedroom home that was owned by an older couple-

Mr. & Mrs. Thomason, who already had 3 foster children living in the house. When I first met them, Ms. Thomason asked me if I was hungry. I said "no", even though I really was. She took me to a room with bunk beds inside and introduced me to three other boys. Their names were Jason, Terell, and Chris. When I sat on the bed, Chris started talking. From that moment, I didn't like him.

Later that night, I started thinking of ways to run away again. The only problem was that I did not know anything yet about the location

I was in. I went to sleep thinking that I was in hell. What I didn't know was that it really was help from above.

Our Help From Above

I Praise You, Heavenly Father, for helping us
When we didn't have a place to stay,
Thank You for protecting and loving us and keeping us in Your grace.
Lord, You have been so merciful and kind and without You we would been left behind. Even when we doubted You,
You made sure ourbellies were fine.
You have loved us and always stayed by our sides. For
You are our protector, who makes sure we don't have to find a place to hide.
With You, we can do anything because You surround us with love,
Father, You are our strength, shield, and our help from above.
Poem by Antonio E. Walker

Way of Life

Our help is from the Lord who made the heavens and the earth.
Psalms 124:8

Prayer

Heavenly Father,

I know I have at times disappointed You, But You still have always been here, In my life. Thank You and I love You so much! You have been so loving and kind towards me. You bless me with Your mercy, And love even when I don't deserve it. You continue to help me in my troubles. Please forgive me for all my sins, Keep me protected, and help me to always stay on The right path to heaven. Holy Father, in Your son Jesus Christ name I pray. Amen!

Chapter Nine

Our Father Knows

Our Father knows what our needs are. He knows we need food, protection, a place to live, love, guidance and many other things. We don't have to worry about our problems; all we have to do is thank Him for always providing for us.

Bread of Life

When you pray don't babble on and on as people of other religions do. They think their prayers are answered only by repeating their words again and again.

Don't be like them, because your father knows exactly what you need even before you ask him!

Matthew 6:7-8

(NLT)

God was Protecting Me

I never imagined that the first two weeks living in foster care would be relaxing and comfortable for me. I still sometimes thought about running away and going back to the streets, but the longer I stayed, the more I liked it.

When I lived with my mom and was running the streets, I knew that selling drugs was wrong; but that was the only thing I trusted to get the money and the things that I wanted.. Being in a foster home had changed my way of thinking a little. For the first time in my life, I trusted something other than selling drugs.

I had everything I needed. Each month the state sent my foster parents around four hundred dollars for each child that was living in their home. This money provided for our clothes, shoes, food etc. That was more than anyone had ever spent on me at any time. I played video games whenever I wanted and ate whatever I wanted. My three foster brothers and I started hanging together. We played football, basketball, and other sports.

I still missed my sisters and mom, but after a while I was allowed to visit my

family. Eventually, my mom got out of jail and my sisters moved back in with my her. When my caseworker asked me if I wanted to go back and live with her, I told him "No!". I loved her and my sisters dearly, but I was tired of living life always in need of things.

I just wanted to be a kid and have fun instead of worrying about where my next meal would come from. I was tired of kids making fun about my clothes and shoes. Now, all I had to do was go to school and stay out of trouble and I would be taken great care of. I decided that I wanted to just relax, chill, and be a child. When I first went into foster care I thought it was because of bad luck, but it was actually God giving me peace and providing for me.

The Heavenly Father Knows

The Heavenly Father knows we have troubles and pain in our life, but he makes sure we don't suffer long and that all hurts are made right.

Healing our cuts, wounds, body, and ripping our doubts apart, not judging us by our actions, but only by our heart.

We were stealing, fighting, killing and destined to be lost, but for our sin he gave his only Son and paid the highest cost.

Wondering if we'll make it and not knowing for sure,

Doctors said we wouldn't but God always found the cure.

Living life in poverty and scared of being to poor; but He sends his blessing abundantly and puts them at our door.

A mighty and caring God who gives us only the best,

When we were tired and couldn't sleep he put our souls to rest.

Things we needed and wanted but chances of getting them were slim,

But our Almighty Father knows what our needs are before we can even pray for them.

Poem by Antonio E. Walker

Way of Life

Talk no more so very proudly;

Let no arrogance come from your mouth;

For the Lord is the God of knowledge; and by him actions are weighed.

1 Samuel2:3

(NKJV)

Prayer

Heavenly Father,

I Thank You for blessing me abundantly. You have always blessed me with the things that I needed and given me the things that I wanted. I praise Your works and Your Holy name, Hallelujah. Thank You for being my God because I don't know where I would be without You. You are very merciful and Your wisdom goes far beyond understanding. Forgive me for not always acknowledging You in my life. Only You deserve my worship and all the glory. Father I love You. In Jesus name I pray.

Amen!

NEW YORK TIMES BESTSELLER
AMAZON PRIME MIND
CONTROLLERS
MEDITATION
Power of THE MIND
How To
TRUMP WORLD
DONALD TRUMP MUST BE STOPPED!!!
#1
CONSPIRACY BOOKS
PRESIDENT DONALD TRUMP IS DESTROYING THE UNITED
PRAISE
POWER
LOTTERY
MANIFESTATION
Powerball Lottery Secrets
WIN
SOUNDS OF
MEDITATION MUSIC
Prosperity

Chapter Ten

GOD IS DIRECTING OUR Paths

We sometimes think situations happen by chance or luck, but that is never the case. The Father is always leading us toward His plan for our lives. We may fall off of His plan for our life. We may fall off of his path, but He will make sure He directs us back because He loves and has a purpose for each and every one of us.

BREAD OF LIFE

We can make our plans but the Lord determines our steps.
Proverbs 16:9

The Lord Was Directing My Path

Living in foster care was living stress free. While with my family, whenever I or my sisters did something wrong we received a whooping or loss of privileges. Foster care was very different. Caseworkers let the children know from the start that if a foster parent put their hands on a child in any way, cuss at a child, or threaten a child to report it to them immediately. I, being 14 and used to getting my butt whooped if I did something crazy, took full advantage of this rule. Letting me know that I couldn't be touched, no matter how horrible I behaved, was only setting me up for trouble.

I started being rebellious to instructions and felt that no one could tell me anything. I started smoking weed and running the streets again with my old friends. My foster parents did not like me hanging around my old friends and used to tell me to stay away from them before I got into a world of trouble. I, thinking I was grown, ignored their advice and continued to hang with my friends anyway.

My foster parents soon got tired of me, and told my caseworker I couldn't stay with them anymore because I was too hard-headed. My caseworker begged them to allow me to stay in their home at least until he could find another home for me. They agreed, and I stayed with them for about another month. Although my caseworker tried to find another family to accept me, he couldn't.

Most foster parents don't like accepting kids over thirteen years old because they feel that teenagers thought they were grown and that most were hardheaded trouble makers who would be a bad influence on the younger kids in the home. So, my caseworker ended up sending me to Atlanta, where I was accepted into an independent living program called The Young Adults Guidance Center. The Y.A.G.C. program teaches young adults independent living skills to help them be on their own in the world.

I found myself stuck in a new and even worse reality. My misbehaving had led me to Atlanta, a city where I knew no one and often felt out of place and alone. Even though I thought it was the worst place I could be, I didn't know God was directing my path.

The Lord Watches and Directs Our Paths

We were falling into a life of regret and darkness, But the Lord was our shephard He kept us safe and protected.

He leads us through the rain, mist, and thick fog, Holding our hand so, if we slip, we shall not fall.

Guiding us towards happiness, peace and eternal life,

The Lord is our guide,

Our light to see in the night.

His love is compassionate and how great is His mercy,

Still blessing us when we are wrong and did things that weren't worthy,

Helping us when we were lost and steering us away from harm,

Taking care of our needs,

And if we were cold keeping us warm.

We are always in His grace when we awake to another day,

The Lord is our protector.

He directs our paths and our way.

Poem by Antonio E. Walker

Way of Life

In all your ways acknowledge him. and He shall direct your paths.
Proverbs 3:5 (NKJV)

Prayer

Thank You Heavenly Father,
For loving me, and blessing me with Your many blessings. You have always kept me protected and directed me away from harm. Please forgive me for falling off of Your path. I trust You in leading me to the life You have planned for me. You are righteous and always faithful to me and I am truly grateful. Please guide me in this life and keep me in Your protection. In Jesus Christ name I pray,
Amen!

Chapter Eleven

Being Willing and Obedient

When we fall off the chosen path of the Lord, we sometimes get discouraged and feel ashamed. We tell ourselves there's no need of praying because we have sinned so much. But don't feed in to that. The Lord has mercy on the willing and looks in our hearts to see if we really want to be obedient. If we are sincere, then He will have patience with us during

our fight with the flesh.

Bread of Life

DON'T YOU REALIZE THAT whatever you choose to obey become your master? You could choose sin, which leads to death, or you can choose to obey God and receive his approval. Thank God! Once you were slaves of sin, but now you have obeyed with all your heart the new

teaching God has given you. Now you are free from sin, your old master, and you have become slaves to your new master, righteousness.

Romans 6:16-18

(NLT)

Willing to Change

Because I was about to turn 15 in a few months, my caseworker helped me get accepted into the Young Adult Guidance Center program. The program was designed to help anyone from the ages of 14 to 22 who did not have goals, independent living skills, employment, and needed help getting a residence. When I moved into YAGC, I did not know what to expect. I was missing my friends back in Columbus, and wished I had moved back in with my mom.

When I arrived at the center, I was introduced to the director- Mr. Simpson. He went over the programs plans, goals, and rules. of their own. The first goal of the program is obtaining employment. Then, you are to set up a bank account in which half of whatever you made was deposited and the other half was split between you and the center. The program was originally designed to last up to 8- 12 months. By then, if the participants had been doing what they were supposed to do, they should have enough money to find their own place to live. Being that I was in foster care, the rules were a little different for me. I had to stay in school, obtain a workers permit, and then find a job. The thing that really got my attention about the program was that all of my money would go to my bank account because foster care paid the center my rent.

I decided that I would give it an honest chance, do my best, and stay out of trouble. And, for about eight months, that is exactly what I did. I went to school, obtained a workers permit, got a job working in a church pantry, and stayed out of trouble and off of drugs. I learned how to ride the Marta bus, do my own Landry, and cook for myself. I was very successful for my age, and had saved a couple thousand dollars. I was willing to change, put my disobedience to the side, and was living an honest life. What surprised me was that I was happy.

Obedient and Willing

We are given by God a free will to do what's right
Or, if we wish, to go down the path of doing wrong.
Most will choose to be disobedient and weak.
But a few will obey and stay strong.
Those who are obedient will get to live a long and prosperous life.
The ones that are rebellious will see their days chopped down
As if cut with a knife.
Some are willing to change, And take help from the Lord hands.
Others harden their hearts,
And carry out their own evil plans, Never listening to advice, and
only judging for themselves,
Then wondering what happened
When they reach their young and early death.
. The wise ones that listen will enjoy wisdom and spiritual healing,
But the only way into this group is to be to God willing and obedi-
ent.

Poem by Antonio E. Walker

Way of Life

If ye be willing and obedient, ye shall eat the good of the land;
but if ye refuse and rebel, ye shall be
devoured with the sword: for the mouth of the Lord hath spoken
it.

Isaiah 1:19-20
(NKJV)

Prayer

Heavenly Father,

You have examined my heart and know everything about me. You know I'm willing to change and want to be obedient to your commands, but my flesh is weak and I need your help. Please lead me, Father and give me the strength to always obey You. I put my life in Your hands and pray for Your guidance. I love You. In Your Holy Son Jesus' name I pray.

Amen!

Following the Wrong People

Following the wrong people will lead us towards destruction. The Bible says that the way of the wicked is like stumbling through complete darkness.

Bread of Life

My child, if sinners entice you, turn your back on them.
Proverbs 1:10
(NLT)

Following the Wrong People

When I was sixteen, I was working at the Waffle House. I had started as a waiter. When the manager saw how the way that the customers took to me and that I was a hard worker, he trained me to be a cook. When I began cooking, I went from making $2.15 an hour plus tips to $8.00 an hour plus tips. The manager explained to me that if I continued to work hard, one day I would be able to be a manager of a restaurant and possibility buy into the franchise. I was still doing well in school and staying out of trouble. Now I had a new goal - to buy my own Waffle House.

Around that same time, an eighteen year old boy named Melvin became my roommate at the center. We found out that we had a lot in common. Like me, Melvin had nowhere to stay and his mom was also addicted to crack cocaine. He had been raised in the Macannyville projects in Atlanta, where he had lived until he had moved in with a married woman who was going through a separation with her husband. The woman had reunited with her husband, leaving Melvin with nowhere to stay.

I talked to my manager and got Melvin a job working with me and we soon became like brothers. Things went well until he talked me into skipping school and work to go hang with his old homeboys in Macannyville. Melvin's friends sold drugs, chased women, drank beer, and smoked marijuana all day. They offered him some beer and marijuana. He accepted and asked me if I wanted some. I really didn't, but everybody was looking at me and I didn't want to seem like a lame, so I accepted. This would become an everyday routine and soon, we both got fired. I didn't care though because, by then, all I wanted to do was drink and smoke.

When the center found out that we had gotten fired and that had been skipping school, they kicked Melvin out of the program. I was also removed from the program and my caseworker was told that he would have to come and get me. I didn't want to lose Melvin because I looked up to him and felt that he was my brother. So, I ran away from the center and went to the projects, where Melvin was living with the once again separated married woman.

I stayed with Melvin and started selling drugs again.

Life, from my point of view at the time, was great. One day Melvin and I were hanging on the corner when he told me to stay there while he ran to the house for a second. I agreed. After about an hour had passed, Melvin still had not returned. I started walking back towards the apartment. As I got closer, I could see police cars and ambulances everywhere. I was a runaway, so I stayed in the back of the crowd. I saw Melvin's girlfriend crying and I got butterfly's in my stomach.

When everyone had cleared, I walked up to the apartment and his girl told me everything. Melvin had returned home and found her husband there. Her husband and Melvin got into an intense argument and started fighting. Her husband pulled out a gun and shot Melvin in the face, killing him instantly. I could not believe it until the day of his wake when I saw him in the casket. Melvin's casket was open, but when you looked closely at his face, it looked like a plastic doll's face.

I cried so hard, I really missed my friend and brother. I stayed with Melvin's girlfriend for about two more months. I began having nightmares and was afraid Melvin's ghost was in her house, so I turned myself in and waited until my caseworker came from Columbus came to get me. True enough, I loved Melvin, but I have to admit that my life was better before I met him.

Follow the Son of God

Following the word of God will
Lead our Souls to joy And let our minds be at ease.
Do not follow wicked friends
Who are evil in their plans and with their Tongues deceive.
Turn your back on them,
Their goal is to trick you
With traps that can lure,
Instead have faith in God without doubt And believe in
something that's pure.
Some people we really don't like
And to some we can give our love away,
But if the way they are living is wrong, Then from them, we
must stay. Jesus is the true Shepherd
And your love is all He demands.
So give up on being led by the blind And let Jesus take your
hand.
Poem by Antonio E. Walker

Way of Life

Then Samuel said to the people,
DO NOT FEAR. YOU HAVE done all this wickedness; yet do not
turn aside from
following the Lord, but serve the Lord with all your heart.
1 Samuel 12:20

(NKJV)

Prayer

Almighty Lord Jesus,

On this blessed day, I pray to You to say thank you for giving Your life for my sake. I'm sorry for following the wrong people, when I should have been following You. I know You are the true Shepherd, and that you will lead me in the right direction because you love me. Please forgive me for all of my sins, all unrighteousness, and also for being very foolish. I repent and accept Your forgiveness and will allow You to lead me into heaven.

I love You, and vow to obey Your Father's commandments. In Your magnificent name I pray.

Amen!

Chapter Thirteen
Living the Fast Life

Living wrong and in the fast life can seem easy, but the cost is extremely steep. We may obtain money, cars, and other expensive material things, but we get trapped in that lifestyle. We give up our happiness and will live uncomfortable, with no peace of mind.

Bread of Life

Whereas ye know not what shall be on tomorrow.
FOR WHAT IS YOUR LIFE? It is a vapor, that appeareth for a little time then vanisheth away. For that ye ought to say if the will, we shall live and

do this, or that. But now ye rejoice in your boastings: all such rejoicing is evil. Therefore to him that

knoweth to do good, and doeth it not, to him it is sin.

James 4:14-17
(KJV)

Living the Fast Life

I was once again living in Columbus, Georgia - my home and really the only place I ever loved. I had started again visiting my mom and sisters. My sisters were doing ok and my mom had stopped using drugs and had even found herself a job. I was living with another foster family and going to night school to get my G.E.D. I had just turned seventeen and was now tired of living in foster care. I felt that I was grown, and that I was capable of living on my own. I told myself all I had to do was sell drugs like I used to do and then I would be able to afford my own place.

So, I ran away from foster care and started selling drugs again. My caseworker couldn't do anything to stop me now because I was of the legal age in Georgia to live on my own. Things started great and soon had saved enough money to rent my own apartment and even bought a car. I was drinking alcohol again and smoking all of the weed I wanted. So, to me, life was good.

I knew I could have found a job easily, but I decided I didn't want to work for anyone other than myself. When I was working at the waffle house I brought home around $250 each week. Now, selling drugs, I easily made that on a slow day. I became content with my new way of living and really thought I had found my true purpose and calling in life. All the people who bought drugs from me loved me and soon built up a steady clientele base. I promised myself that I would never work a legit job again as long as drugs were available. I was a drug dealer and that was what I wanted to be for the rest of my life. I loved and enjoyed my exciting occupation and soon became addicted to making fast money and living the fast life.

Life Is Too Short

Life is too short to be trying to live it too fast,

So take it one day at a time and try to make it last.

But live it in a honest way and strive for the best,

And give your life to the almighty Lord, and let him do the rest.

Grow up, mature and stop playing childish games,

And start living as adults praying to make it to a older age.

Our true purpose is to serve and worship God our creator who has never left us alone.

0r Life will fly by us and before we know what happened Our days on earth will be gone.

When we praise and glorify the Lord

He will protect us with his powerful might,

And trusting in him will win every battle and all fights.

When we are here we are here and when we are gone were gone,

But choose to live in the right way,

And God will let us live forever With Him in His Heavenly home.

Poem by Antonio E. Walker

Way of Life

MY CHILD LISTENS TO me and does as I say, and you will have along, good life. I will teach you wisdoms ways and lead you in straight paths. If you live a life

guided by wisdom, you won't limp and stumble as you run. Carry out my instructions; don't forsake them.

Guard them, for they will lead youto a fulfilled life.

Proverbs 4:10-13

Prayer

Heavenly Father,

I pray to You in Your Son, Jesus Christ's name.

I ask for forgiveness of all my sins. I repent from them and will start living in the ways of the wise. Please slow me down Lord and show me the way.

Let Your will be done in my life. I know I have been living in a way that is dishonest and have disappointed You many times, but I don't want to continue living like this. I need You and my Lord Jesus Christ. Please help me and give me strength so that I can start making the right decisions for my life. In Jesus holy name I pray.

Amen!

Chapter Fourteen

Ill Gotten Gains

Wealth from get-rich-quick schemes quickly disappears; Wealth from hard work grows.

Bread of Life

And the Lord says;
Behold therefore, I beat my fists at the dishonest profit which you
have made, and at the bloodshed which has been in your mist.
Ezekiel 22:13
(NKJV)

I Lost Everything

One morning, a couple of guys and I were on the corner selling drugs, when, out of nowhere, the police rode up, jumped out of their cars, and started chasing us. Being that I'm not athletic and can't run that fast, I got caught and searched. While running, I had managed to get rid of the drugs that were on me. I was still taken to jail for obstruction and loitering. On the way to the prescient, I started thinking about all of the stories I had heard. I got very scared and soon I began to cry. I didn't know my bail was only going to be around $200. All I could think about was being beaten up or raped. When we arrived at the jail, I was processed and told my bail. I had around $500 on me and paid the bail immediately.

When I was released, I called a cab and then went home. I was very happy to be out and told myself I would never stand on a street corner selling drugs again. I went to the store, bought a pager, and gave all of my customers my number. Whenever a customer paged me, I would meet them at a store or restaurant. I soon got tired of meeting customers and told them to just come by my apartment instead of a neutral location.. I didn't know at the time that one of the most important rules selling drugs was to not sell where you laid your head.

I had around twenty-five customers who would come by my apartment and spend large quantities of money with me. I started saving large sums of money. The best part about it was that I didn't have to leave my apartment or go anywhere.

I got hungry one day, and decided to go out and buy something to eat. When I returned home, I noticed a lot of people standing around my apartment. I didn't know what was going on until I noticed that the back of their shirts read Metro Narcotics. Some of them were inside of my apartment, so I just continued to ride on by without being noticed. Everything I owned and all the money I had saved was in the apartment. I knew I couldn't go back. I just kept on riding until I found someone with I.D. and paid them to rent me a hotel room with the little money I had left in my pocket. When I settled into the room, I lay on the bed and tried to think of my next move. I had lost basically everything I owned. All I had left was a couple hundred dollars. I went to sleep thinking I would just start over, but what I didn't know was that it was going to be a lot harder than I thought.

Ill Gotten Gains

When times get difficult
WE SOMETIMES BECOME frustrated and discouraged, And choose the wrong but easiest way out.

We don't want to be patient and work hard, So we find a decoy and go the most dangerous route.

Dishonesty, violence and greed
Are just a few of the things that will set in, Not living our lives in a honorable fashion And a burden to our family and friends.

Instead of having faith in Jesus
And following all of his commands, We decide to follow our wicked desires

And chase our own foolish get rich quick plans.

Christ is always helping us in our struggles
And even in the days when nothing seems to be going our way.

So put your trust in Jesus
Because he will save us and lead us to a brighter day.

The devil will always tempt us And when we are weak
He will fog and blind our sight,

But pray for correction and protection And Start living for the glory of the Lord, And begin to live your life in a way that's right.

Poem by Antonio E. Walker

Way of Life

Ill gotten gain has no lasting value, but right living can save your life.
The Lord will not let the Godly
starve to death, but he refuses to satisfy the craving of the wicked.
Proverbs 10:2-3
(NLT)

Prayer

Almighty Jesus,

Forgive me for being stubborn and stuck in my wicked ways. I have been trying to please my worldly desires instead of You and have hurt people along the way to obtain money and other materialistic things. I have loved and put my selfishness before Your commandments and I pray for Your forgiveness and mercy. Please take over my needs. I trust in You from this day forth to take over my life. I know and believe I can be prosperous in a way that pleases You and God, in Your name I pray,

Amen!

Chapter Fifteen
We Reap What We Sow

If we sow good seeds, then we will receive the blessings if the Lord, but if we sow evil seeds then we are choosing the road that leads to death.

Bread of Life

Even as I have seen, those who plow inquiry and sow trouble reap the
same. By the blast of God they perish, and by the breath of his anger
they are consumed.
Job 4:8-9
(NKJV)

Planting the Wrong Seeds

I was scared to go back to my apartment, so I was living in my car and barely making it. I probably could have gone back home and lived with my mom and sisters, but my pride would not allow me to. I told myself to just tough it out and everything would be ok.

I still had my car, pager, and my customers; but it just wasn't the same anymore. Now whenever they paged me, I again had to meet them at a store or restaurant. When I was selling out of my apartment I was making five times more money than working off my pager. I learned that drug smokers liked having the drugs brought to them or going to the dealer's home instead of having to go to a street corner to buy drugs. My new goal was to get another apartment so that I could start making the big money I was accustomed to.

One day, while I was on my way to serve one of my customers, I ran into a road block and had to jump out of my car. I tried to out run the police and at the same time throw out the crack cocaine that I had in my possession, but they caught me and searched the area. At first, I did not think that they would find the drugs, but they were very persistent and searched for about an hour. They finally found what they were looking for. They arrested me and took the little bit of money I had in my pocket and my car.

Now I really had nothing. I was charged with possession of cocaine, booked and taken upstairs. When I was selling drugs I never took any time to think about what would happen to me if I ever got caught. All I thought about at the time was the great money that I was making. Not once did I think about how I used to feel when I saw my own mother using drugs or how I was selling them to someone else's family members and hurting them. I never thought about the consequences my actions would bring. The seeds that I had planted in my life were growing and eventually I ended up reaping what I had sown.

We Reap What We Sow

Doing good deeds is living for our mighty savior Jesus Christ,
We will be blessed with love, protection, guidance And living for
ever with Him in eternal life.
But if we are wicked and disobedient
It is our blessings we will be stealing,
Life will be confusing and painful
Because we are missing out on our spiritual healings.
When we listen to correction and wisdom
We plant seeds of enlightenment and understanding
Following the ways of the wise we turn from our sins,
But when we are blind and foolish doing all the evil we can,
Chances of going to heaven become slim.
So be very careful what you do
And watch the way you speak, Because whatever we choose to do Is
what our souls are going to reap.
Poem by Antonio E. Walker

Way of Life

Don't be mislead. Remember that you can't ignore God and get away with it. You will always reap what you sow. Those who live only to satisfy their own

sinful desires will harvest the consequences of decay and death. But those who live to please the spirit will harvest everlasting life.

Galatians 6:7-8

(NLT)

Chapter Sixteen Overcoming Selfishness

When we are blessed by God with success and riches, it is His will that we share with others. We cannot let greed or selfishness stop us from doing what we should - treating others as we would like to be treated. When we are in need, the Lord makes sure we get what we are in need of. We should show the same love towards others in need.

Bread of Life

Tell those who not to be proud and not to trust in their money, which will soon be gone. But their trust should be in the living God, who richly gives us all we need for our enjoyment. Tell them to use their

money to do good. They should be rich in good works

and should give generously to those in need, always be ready to share with others whatever God has given them. By doing this they will be storing up their

treasure as a good foundation for the future so that they may take hold of real life.

1 Timothy 6:17-19

(NLT)

All for Myself

I had just turned 19 when I finished my 8 months of incarceration. I had served four months at the Muscogee county jail and four months in boot camp. When I got released, I was given a $35 check, a pair of brown slacks, and a white long sleeved collared dress shirt. A long-time friend of mine named Anthony asked his mom if I could stay with them and she was kind enough to accept me into her home.

I was on three years of probation and was given two months to find a job. When I went back to the projects, a dealer I knew gave me a gram of crack and told me to get back on my feet. This was all that I had at the time to my name. I took that gram of crack and flipped it until I had saved enough money to buy an ounce, and from there I never looked back. I told myself that I was going to save every penny I made and that's just what I did.

I didn't have any clothes and I wanted another place of my own. I continued to save until I had enough money for an apartment. Then I started recruiting new customers. I couldn't use marijuana anymore, so now I was making a lot more money than before. After a month had gone by, I counted the money I had been saving. I had thirteen thousand dollars. That was the most money I had ever seen or had at one time. I went out and bought a car, clothes, and a mouth full of gold teeth.

No one could tell me that I wasn't the man. Women definitely noticed my success and started throwing themselves at me. I went and saw my family and took my sisters out shopping for new shoes and gave my mom some money. Life for me was once again great. I didn't think about the fact that I had just being released from incarceration. I was now making big money and I credited myself for all of my success.

I didn't want to get a job and live a normal life

Our Heavenly Deeds

Be rich in your good works
And please do not be deceive,
Give your hand to anyone who needs assistance, And help all those
who are in need.
Put away selfish acts and repent from
Your evil and wicked doings, Because we can't be all for ourselves
Or we will end up falling into the devils ruins.
Love is all it takes and is the most precious gift
That we can give,
So adopt a generous nature that will lead us Into eternal life with
Christ where we will live.
Have strength for your neighbors
And keep strong for the hard times that are ahead,
Because if we have faith without works,
Then what blessings we had coming to us
Will be given to those who
Take heed to these words instead.
Any wise person with understanding knows
That it is better to give then to receive,
So stop being selfish and live
To bless others with works And do your heavenly deeds.
Poem by Antonio E. Walker

Way of Life

Let no one seek his own, but one the other's well being.
1Corinthians 10:24 (NKJV)

Prayer

Heavenly Father,

I COME TO YOU TODAY before Your holy throne praying for Your mercy. I have been selfish in my ways and also towards others. Please forgive me In the precious name of Your Son Jesus Christ for this sin and the rest of them. Help me to go from this day forth treating everyone as I would like to be treated myself. In Jesus name I pray.

Amen!

Chapter Seventeen
Avoiding False Teachings

Those false teachers who are so anxious to win your favor are not doing it for your good. They are trying to shut you off from me, so that you will pay more attention to them. Galations 4:17(NLT)

Bread of Life

Now the spirit expressly says that in latter times some will depart from
the faith, giving head to deceiving spirits and doctrines of demon.
1 Timothy 4:1

Learning from the Wrong People

I was twenty-one when my life took a drastic turn as a drug dealer. I had around $18,000 saved at the time. Some people would say that wasn't nearly enough to be content with, but most black people from the slums would call that ghetto rich, especially at the age of twenty-one. I was selling drugs out of my house and living the way that I thought I wanted.

At the time I was buying my crack from a friend of mine who was around my age. He had a cousin who was a real heavy weight in the game. His cousin would credit him whatever amount of cocaine that he wanted. Soon he got busted by the Feds and received a sentence to serve 180 months in Federal prison. Being that

he would sometimes take me with him to re-up on more drugs, his cousin soon started treating me the same way. He only dealt in powder cocaine and didn't want to cook my cocaine for me, so he taught me how to cook it myself. From there, I took off.

When a dealer buys his drugs in crack form, he will have to pay at least $700.00 an ounce. But if he knows how to cook it himself, he can buy an ounce of powder and cook it into double easily. And that's exactly what I did. The first package that my friend fronted me was nine ounces of powder cocaine which was going at the time for $6500. I cooked it up myself and ended up with a total of 16 ounces, which I then broke it down into nothing but little rocks. I made around $1200 an ounce doing this. When I had sold it all, in only a week, and counted my money I had around $18,000. I had made a profit of around $11,000 in one week! Now, it was definitely trouble for a twenty-one year old man to be making that much money in a week.

I started buying any and everything wanted. Women that had to have been out of a model magazine were all trying to get my action. My supplier was proud of me and told me that I was on my way to being a young millionaire. The funny thing about that was that I actually believed his every word.

False Teachings

Beware of the teachings of those who are wicked
And whose tongues are quick to tell lies,
For their goals are to lead us to destruction And they teach with formulas that are unwise.
Follow only the Godly and those whose faith
You can see in their good works, They live in the glory of Christ Jesus
And their will is to heal all who are hurt.
But the devil is very persistent
And he's always trying to send his followers our way,
So make sure that you stay cautious
And please never forget that we should pray.
We don't have to worry about being fooled
Or taught and lead by the blind,
Because you will know if their teachings are pure By the way that their acts of love shine.
Some teachers enlighten with words that
Are powerful, honest, and reaching,
But others are evil and deceitful
And out of their mouth comes nothing but false Teaching.
Poem by Antonio Walker

Way of Life

THESE FALSE TEACHERS are like unthinking animals, creatures of instinct, who are both to be caught and

killed. They laugh at the terrifying powers they know so little about, and they will be destroyed along with them. Their destruction is their reward for the harm they have done. They love to indulge in evil pleasure in broad daylight. They are a disgrace and a stain

among you. They reveal in deceitfulness while they

lust is never satisfied. They make a game of luring

unstable people into sin. They train themselves to be greedy; they are doomed and cursed.

2 Peter 2:12-14
(NLT)

Prayer

Almighty Lord Jesus,

I pray to You for protection from false words, false wisdom, and false teachers. I need You Lord to lead me, and to know what is true from what is false. Many people have been trying to teach me things that I know are not right but some of them Im not sure. The only way I can truly know is through You. I love You and thank You for letting me know the difference. In Your name I pray.

Amen!

Chapter Eighteen
Loving an Immoral Women

A WORTHY WIFE IS HER husband's joy and crown. A shameful wife saps his strength.
  Proverbs 12:4(NLT)

Bread of Life

My son pay attention to my wisdom; listen carefully to my wise counsel. Then you will learn to be discreet

and will store up knowledge. The lips if an immoral woman are as sweet as honey, and her mouth is smoother than oil. But the result is as bitter as

poison, sharp as a double-edged sword. Her feet go

down to death: her steps lead straight to the grave.

For she does not care about the path to life. She staggers down a crooked trail and doesn't even realize where it leads.

Proverbs 5:1-6

(NLT)

BLINDLY IN LOVE WITH the Wrong Woman

For most of my life, I have been shy and selfconscience about my looks. With that being said, I could count on half a hand the number of girlfriends that I had in my lifetime. I'm not a fly speaker and I get very nervous just looking at a beautiful woman. But with all the money that I was now making, I didn't have to have the gift of gab to pull a woman. They didn't mind doing all of the talking.

I remember meeting what I thought was one of the most beautiful woman I had ever seen in my life. Her name was Stephanie. I never believed in love at first sight, but I fell in love with her the very first time I laid eyes on her. She was what we called a redbone with curves and weight in all of the right places. I met Stephanie through girlfriend of a friend of mine. I told myself that I would give anything to be her man.

Growing up in a house full of girls I watched movies like Poetic Justice, Jason's Lyrics, and other romantic films all the time. Afterwards, I would daydream and fantasize about finding a beautiful woman and promised myself that I would treat her better than any other man ever could. When I saw Stephanie, I started doing whatever I thought I needed to do to capture her love. If that meant me going broke, then the soup line was where I was headed.

I would end up being deeply in love with her and still have some sort of affection for her to this day. I don't believe I will ever care for another woman the way that I cared for her. I used to believe all of her lies and fell for all of her tricks. I was very naïve and gullible. I really thought at the time that she cared for me in the same way. I once heard someone say that a man who is like putty in a woman's hand will never amount to anything. Well I am a living witness, participant, and believer that this statement is very true.

Chapter Nineteen # Walking on a Thin Line

We need to beware of God's wrath and anger. Our Father in heaven is a patient, loving, and powerful God. When we continue to harden our hearts towards his commandments, He will have no other choice but

to discipline and correct us.

Bread of Life

But while the meat was still between their teeth, before it was chewed, the wrath of the Lord was

aroused against the people, and the Lord struck the people with a very great plague.

Numbers 11:33

(NKJV)

Walking a Thin Line

Everything I ever dreamed of having I either had or was within my grasp. I had cars, plenty of money, a beautiful woman, and power and respect. I had just turned twenty-five and, besides going to prison a few times, was really for the enjoying my life. Steph and I had been on and off for five years, but most of them were splendid.

One day, I was going way to sell drugs to a friend of mine. I pulled up and parked in front of his house. I got out of the car and knocked on his door. He answered and I walked into his home. He wanted to purchase two and a half ounces of crack cocaine. I had brought him seventy-four grams worth of crack, which was a little over since he was one of my best customers.

While my friend was counting out the money to pay me for the drugs, someone knocked on the door. It was the police. I nervously looked at my friend hoping that someone was just joking, but when he peeped out the window and told me that it real. all that hope was gone. We instantly started to panic. My friend quickly handed the drugs to a crack head that was living with him at the time and took off running out the back door of the house. I was hesitant to run out the back door thinking that the police were certainly in the back yard if they were in the front. But when I peeped out the back door I was shocked to see that they had not surrounded the house. I ran out of the house, but I didn't know the area well.

The police eventually canvassed the area and someone informed them that I had run up under a house. I was caught. My friend had got away. The crack head and I were taken to jail, charged with trafficking of cocaine, and held without bond. I remember thinking to myself that I was dreaming and that none of this was really happening. I pinched myself and realized that the situation was reality.

All I could think about was that I was going to be leaving my girlfriend for a long time. I'm not a snitch, so I wasn't going to tell on any one else, especially when I was in the wrong. I was prepared to do whatever time was given to me without bringing anyone down with me. I know now that I was foolish and walking a very thin line. I was making God very angry with my lifestyle and He showed this by bringing his wrath upon me.

Walk on a Thin Line

There's a war within our spirit,
A battle between both sides,
One helps us to stay holy and honest
But the other is deceitful, wicked
And keeps our heart filled with pride.
To win we must submit
And give our lives over to Christ.
But losing is a massive loss,
A waste of our fathers precious sacrifice.
We are given a will
That's free to chose to do what's good Or things that are not.
But if we keep giving into sinful desires,
We will face punishment Like the evil people did In the story about Lot.
Listen to instruction and stay obedient
Never closing your ears to wisdom
And live to get wise,
For when we don't quit sinning
We are making our Lord angry And walking on a very thin line.
Poem by Antonio E. Walker

WAY OF LIFE

But God shows his anger from heaven against all sinful wicked people who push the truth away from

themselves. For the truth about God is known to them instinctively. God has put this knowledge in their hearts.

Romans 1:18-19

(NLT)

Prayer

Heavenly Father,

I pray to you for forgiveness and mercy. I have sinned and been living in a way that's wrong. I know I have been disobedient and have constantly angered You. I ask to be cleansed through the blood that Your Son Jesus Christ shed for me. Please forgive me and help me to live the right way. I love You Heavenly Father and thank You for Your patience. In Jesus Christ name I pray.

Amen!

Chapter Twenty
Love Someone Who Loves Us More

Jesus replied "what does the law of Moses say? How do you read it?" The man answered. "you must love the Lord your God with all your heart, all your soul, all your strength and all your mind."
Luke 10:26-27 (NLT)

Bread of Life

For God so loved the world that He gave his only begotten son, so that everyone that believes in him, will not perish, but have eternal life.
John 3:16
(NLT)

Loving the Wrong Person

I had served 80 days in the county jail when, suddenly, my lawyer got all my charges dismissed and thrown out of court. I had prayed prayers from the book of Psalms and constantly asked the Lord to forgive me and have mercy on me. He answered my prayer and I was released. The police didn't have a search warrant and all charges were dismissed. I thanked God and credited my release to my constant fasting and prayers.

Stephanie, my love and soul mate (at least that's what I thought she was), had completely deserted me. I was depressed and brokenhearted. Thank the Lord I didn't leave all the money I'd saved in her possession, or I wouldn't have had anything. She never wrote me once, or came to see me when I was locked up. When I called our old house phone, the number had been changed. I couldn't believe she did me like that. I loved her with all my heart, but I found out that she never loved me, just my money.

I got out, only to learn Step had gotten pregnant by a bigger drug dealer than me. I never felt pain in my heart like I did when my sister told me that news. I wondered what I did wrong and couldn't find the answer. I had put all of my heart and trust into that girl and she just spit in my face and never looked back. I wasn't wise enough to see who had always had my back and was looking out for me when I was locked up - God! The Lord spared me with His mercy, and took what I didn't need and the person who I was loving more than Him out of my life. I loved a woman who didn't love me, when I should of been putting all my trust and love in someone who always loved me more than I could ever love Him - the Almighty God.

All Our Hearts

Love the Lord with all your hearts.
Never let anyone or thing come before his glory.
Give praise, prayers, and worship to Him
Because He will heal all pain and takes away all worry.
Release and give Him control over your lives.
Whether you are young or blessed to be old,
Authority and great power is God's, Let His spirit work in your body And let it reach your soul.
His love for us is breath taking and cannot be measured
Because its distance goes on for uncountable length,
Choose to love Him in the same fashion
And live to glorify Him with every ounce of your strength.
Our Lord is a caring and loving Father
Who we should acknowledge
With the wholeness of heart
And keep Him in all the thoughts that we think,
And continue to show appreciation
Because God's love for us has never shrieked.
Poem by Antonio E. Walker

Way of Life

Therefore you shall love the Lord your God, and keep his charge,
his statues, his judgments, and his commandments always.

Deuteronomy 11:2

(NKJV)

Prayer

O merciful Heavenly Father,

I pray on this day in the name of Your Son Jesus Christ. I thank You for Your unconditional love. You have blessed me abundantly with your many blessings and I love You with all of my heart. In the future from this day forth, I promise to be willing and obedient to Your commands. I love You and will start giving You all of my love like I should have always done.In Jesus name I pray.

Amen!

Chapter Twenty-one

Only God Can Judge Us

When people make degrading remarks towards us, we tend to shy away from them, but have strength and turn to the Lord who loves us unconditionally. We may wonder why we suffer and have shameful feelings, but just pray to our God and ask for restoration of joy and peace in your life. Because only He can judge us.

Bread of Life

Disregarding another person's faults preserves love;
Telling about them separates close friends. A single rebuke does more
for a person of understanding than a hundred lashes on the back of a
fool.
Proverbs 17:9-10
(NLT)

Only God Can Judge Me

With plenty of money still saved and while mending my broken heart, I stopped selling drugs for a little while. I used to pray and thank the Lord for being kind enough to allow me to beat my trafficking case, especially since we both knew that I was guilty and caught dead in the act. I also prayed and asked Jesus for forgiveness of all my sins. I told Him that if He would allow me to get my soul mate back, then I would change my life and stop selling drugs for good.

At first, when I got released from jail, I still went around my friends and family, but I eventually shied away from their company and constantly degrading remarks. All of a sudden, everyone seemed to think that they were some wise guru or something. They would say things about Stephanie like "she was just a gold digger", "she never loved you", "she couldn't even stay down with you for 80 days", "You should of known", and, the most popular, "I told you so". It use to hurt my heart every time someone made a remark about Step. Now don't get me confused when I say I know most of their comments were just I knew that they weren't trying to hurt my feelings and that my close family and friends felt sorry for me. They just didn't want me to mess with her again in anyway.

Back then I had only been in love with one woman and I knew deep in my heart that I would do anything for chance to be back with her, pregnant and all. I soon was too ashamed to face the harsh but mostly true remarks from my family and friends. I didn't like the way I felt whenever they said something about her, so I just stayed in the house and smoked marijuana all day. My friends would call me and ask me what I was getting into. I would say I was sick or already had other things planned. I was tired of them judging me. I felt like a fool, a failure, and just wanted to be left alone.

Open the Blinds

Disregard anyone's shortcomings or faults, we all have come up short

when standing next to the glory of our Lord. For everyone has sin with disobedience and has fallen from our mighty Father commandments and holy accord.

This will be hard for proud people who think they are so educated and wise.

You should take a look in the mirror because no one is perfect,
for the Lord despises those
whose hearts are not compassionate but instead are filled with pride.

When people are confused or foolish we should show and teach them the ways of the wise.

So help others who are in the dark and shed some light on their lives,

for the Lord is merciful to those who are helpful to those who can't see and are willing to get and open the blinds.

Poem by Antonio E. Walker

Way of Life

DO NOT SPEAK EVIL OF one another, brethren. He who speaks evil of a brother and judges his brother, speaks evil of the law and judges the law, you are not a doer of the law but a judge.

James 4:11
(NKJV)

Chapter Twenty-two
Revenge is the Lords

When people hurt us, we tend to want to get revenge. But don't re-pay a wrong with a wrong. Instead
forgive them and turn the matter over to God.

Bread of Life

The Lord lives! Blessed be my rock: May God of my salvation be exalted! He is the God who pays back those who harm me.

Psalm 18:46-47

(NLT)

I Was Going to Show the World

One day I was at home playing my video games and eating. At the time this was all I had the desire to do. I had been avoiding everyone and didn't even answer my phone. I was mad at the world and also myself for being so naive. I started thinking about all the love I had been showing Step. I told myself "I'll show her, all I have to do is stack up my money and stunt on her and everyone else that was laughing at me behind my back." I decided I did not want to hide anymore, I wanted revenge. An older cat once told me that money was the best revenge, and that's exactly what I planned to do, stack it to the ceiling and shine like the sun.

I devised a plan. The first step was to find a house and tell all my customers the location. I got into my car and went looking for a new place. It didn't take long for me to find a three bedroom house around the hood. I then called all of my old and some new customers and told them my new location. Then I bought nine ounces of powder cocaine and instead of cooking and stretching it to my usual sixteen ounces, I kept it pure and only cooked ten. I broke down a half ounce into little rocks and passed them out as samples. Because of its purity I eventually sewed up the hood.

On a slow day I sold four and a half ounces and seven on a fast day. I didn't sell in weight; this was sold in little five and ten dollar rocks. I was getting major, major paper. I had a huge chip on my shoulder and I never spent more than a $100 a day, even though I was sometimes making a $3000 profit. I saved every dime. I was determined to get the last laugh over step everyone else that was laughing at me.

Revenge is the Lords

Sometimes getting revenge seems to be
The best and only way,
But please don't participate in any wrong doing But let the Lord do
the repaying.
Forgiving will be hard when we don't have mercy And understanding
in our hearts.
So let the Lord have his glory And let his power do its part. He will
avenge us surely
And even up all of the scores.
For He's a just Father and His children He adores.
We must be patient to let our God take the situation
And the problem in His place
Because if someone ties knots in our shoes,
Our Lord will unloosen them and straighten up the lace.
When people are successful
With bringing hurt upon our life.
The Lord will avenge all who have been done wrong,
And bring His anger and strife in His might.
Poem by Antonio E. Walker

Way of Life

Dearly beloved, avenge not yourselves, but rather give place unto wrath: for it is written, vengeance is mine: I will repay, says the Lord.

Romans 12:19

(KJV)

Prayer

Heavenly Father,

Don't let my enemy gloat over me or rejoice at my downfall. I am on the verge of collapse, facing constant pain. But I confess my sins; I am deeply sorry for what I have done. My enemies are many; They hate me though I have done nothing against them. They repay me even evil for good and oppose me because I stand for right. Do not abandon me, Lord. Do not stand at a distance, my God. Come quickly to help me, O Lord my Savior. In Jesus Christ name I pray.

Amen!

Psalms 35:16-22 (NLT)

Chapter Twenty-three

Hardening Our Hearts Toward Others

BUT IF ANYONE HAS ENOUGH money to live well and sees a brother or sister in need and refuses to help-how can God's love be in that that person?

 1 John 3:17(NLT)

Bread of Life

Happy is the man who is always reverent, But he who hardens his
heart will fall into calamity.
Proverbs 28:14
(NKJV)

Treating Others with Kindness

We have to treat one another with kindness
    Because that is what's right and the Godly thing to do.
Showering each other with love,
So that our father can see that our hearts are really clean and pure.
Helping anyone we can and not forgetting to show them the Bibles plan,
Which consists of living life forever in heaven Singing our God's praises together Thanking him and holding hands.
    Poem by Antonio E. Walker

Way of Life

If I could speak in any language in heaven or on earth but didn't love others, I would only be making meaningless noise like a loud gong or a clanging

cymbal. If I had the gift of prophecy, and if I knew all the mysteries of the future and knew everything about everything, but didn't love others, what good

would I be? And if I had the gift of faith so that I

could speak to a mountain and make it move, without love I would be of no good to anybody. If I gave

everything I had to the poor and even sacrificed my body, I could boast about it; but if I didn't love others, I would be of no value what-soever.

1 Corinthians 13:1-3

(NLT)

Prayer

Heavenly Father,

I pray that You forgive me for hardening my heart towards others, grant me the serenity to accept the things I cannot change, the courage to change the things I can, and the wisdom to know the difference. In Jesus Christ name I pray.

Amen!

Chapter Twenty-four
We Always Need Discipline

WHEN WE WERE CHILDREN, we didn't want to be punished or corrected for anything. But as we got older, we were glad that our parents loved us enough to discipline us. We need guidance until we leave this earth. Our Father which are in heaven will correct us and make sure He puts us in our place if we step out of line. And he does this all because he loves and

wants what's best for us.

Bread of Life

To learn, you must love discipline; it is stupid to hate correction. The Lord approves of those who are Good, but he condemns those who plan wickedness.

Proverbs 12:1-2
(NLT)

I Needed Correction

A "trap" is what drug dealers call a house that is used to sell drugs. It's called a trap because that's what it really is. If a drug dealer is selling drugs on a street corner, there are plenty of ways that he could run and get away from the police and throw or stash the drugs that he has in his possession. If he is in a trap house the police or drug task force know exactly where to find him and will strategize ways to capture him inside. That's why most drug dealers like to always stay on the move. A moving target is hard to hit and capture.

The money made selling from a street corner isn't comparable to that of selling from a trap house. When people know where they can go and get a product that is good in quality and quantity, they will come flocking just as they do when they go to a McDonalds or Burger King. And that is exactly what I thought that I had, a baby McDonalds. But because of the constant traffic of people coming and quickly leaving from my trap, the location became extremely hot and the police started riding up and down the streets in front of my house daily. Me being foolish and naïve, I never thought about my surroundings.

The police were trying to catch a customer leaving my house by waiting until they walked or drove around the corner to pull them over and search them for drugs. If the police found drugs on the users they would give them two choices. Either set up whoever they purchased the drugs from or go to jail. I thought that I knew all there was to know about selling drugs and life in general. I ignored all of the signs and warnings that God was giving me to quit while I was ahead and continued right on selling drugs. I had my doors bolted down like Fort Knox and thought that all I needed was enough time to get rid of the drugs inside of my house if the police ever came.

When the drug task force came and shot tear gas inside of my trap, I was stunned and taken by surprise. I managed to flush the drugs, but the police had a warrant for my arrest for sale of cocaine. They arrested me and asked if I wanted to help myself by setting up another drug dealer. I refused their proposal and was instantly taken to jail. The next morning I went to court and the judge denied my bond.

I went back inside my jail cell and looked at the sky. I started screaming and yelling at God. I told Him that He didn't love me because, out of all the drug dealers out on the street selling drugs and getting away with it, I had gotten caught. He decided to punish me - a boy whose life was messed up from the beginning. I didn't know then what I know now - that God disciplines those He loves and all the ones that He accepts as his children.

WE ALWAYS NEED DISCIPLINE

Being corrected is something
That we must desire,
Look foward to,
Hunger for in our hearts And always cherish.
We shouldn't ignore
When the Lord corrects us And continue to do wrong,
If we want to have eternal life.
We must live in a way
That's pleasing to the Lord
So that our spirits will never have to perish.
There is no one on this earth
That doesn't need to be guided And no one that is wise enough
That they don't have to pay attention.
So accept Jesus as your personal Christ and Savior
And He will help you to complete your earthly missions.

Our parents tried to instruct us,
But there were times when we wouldn't take heed
Or just chose not to listen,
But the Lord will punish all those Who are his children
And corrects them through his love And with much discipline.
Poem by Antonio E. Walker

Way of Life

And have you entirely forgotten the encouraging words God spoke to
you, his children? My child don't
ignore it when the Lord disciplines you, and don't be discouraged
when he corrects you. For the Lord
disciplines does he loves, and He punishes those he accepts as his children.
Hebrews 12:5-6 (NLT)

Prayer

Our Father which are in heaven,
HALLOWED BE THY NAME, thou kingdom come, thou will be done on earth as it is in heaven. Give us this day our daily bread and forgive us for our trespasses as we forgive those who trespass against us, Lead us not into temptation but deliver us from evil. For thou is the kingdom, the power, and the glory, forever and ever, In Jesus Christ name we pray.

Amen!

Bread of Life

The Lord is my light and my salvation; Whom shall I fear? The Lord is the strength of my life; Of whom shall I be afraid? When the wicked came against me to eat up my flesh, my enemies and foes, They stumbled and fell. Though an army may encamp against me, My heart shall not fear; Though war may rise against me, In this I will be confident.

Psalms 27:1-3

(NKJV)

Black Panther Inspiration? Within You there is Strength

The cost of growing up in a poor family is poverty. The reward for knowing how to pray is priceless. That's the one thing, besides love and birth, that my mother gave to me. If my family and I ate three meals a day it was truly a blessing from God. Life on welfare is barely manageable, but trying to live life on welfare when your mom is addicted to drugs is almost like trying to breathe under water. Growing up my life may have been difficult, but I have to take credit for bring a large part of trouble upon myself. I always felt weak inside whether it was low self esteem, talking to my peers, my abilities, or my financial situations.

I always prayed and asked God "Why not me?". Why wasn't I blessed with a rich family, good looks or an athletic frame? Why were people always downing, talking about, and criticizing me? Why couldn't I be successful at anything I did? Why wasn't I blessed with talents? Why do I always feel weak and depressed and get my feelings hurt? Why was I put on this earth? Was I born to suffer?

This form of thinking is what lead me to where I am now - in prison. I am currently serving a sentence of 12 years for sale of cocaine. I grew up thinking I was born to be punished. For what I had no idea, but felt I must have done something to be cursed. I never was happy until I started selling drugs, at least that's what I thought. when I was selling drugs I made plenty of money, but the most addictive thing about it was the attention I got from others. No one noticed me until I started buying cars, clothes, and jewelry. Women gave me the attention I desire for. They would seduce me and would tell me anything and everything I could ever dream of hearing.

I did not know that I was setting myself up for a life of misery, heartache, and plenty of days of loneliness. Seventy-five percent of the women that date drug dealers are only with them for the money. Some refer to these women as gold diggers. I came to like and date quite a few, but whenever I went to jail they left me. I would be in jail, lonely, broken hearted, and all alone. This would go on for majority of my life.

I can honestly say I liked a lot of women, but few of them liked me back, they only liked what I could do for them at the time. The same can be said about many of my so-called friends. When I was out on the streets, they would have my back, but when times got rough and I got locked up they never wrote to see how I was doing, or sent me any money. The only people that cared were my family and God. God softened and humbled my families' hearts and they continue to love me even though when I was on the streets. I didn't love and care for them the way that I knew I was supposed to.

I am tired of living the life that I have been living. I'm currently in Smith State Prison located in Glennville, Georgia. If you look it up on the internet you will see that it is one of the most violent prisons in the state of Georgia. When I first came here I couldn't believe my luck. I'm surrounded by prisoners who are never going home, who will stab you for looking at them wrong. I'm considered weak, or lame because I don't want to stab or hurt someone and because I stay away from other prisoners that like to rob or kill.

It goes back to what I was saying earlier, the one thing I am truly thankful my mom gave to me was to gift of knowing how to pray. The Lord protects me from many of these prisoners that are demon possessed. I use to be afraid of them until I found strength from His word. Through much prayer, I now know that he loves unconditionally everyday and sent me here to change my ways and to show me what selling drugs would lead to. I know without a shadow of a doubt that I don't want to live around killers and robbers for the rest of my life. I'm tired of missing my nieces and nephews growing up. I'm tired of selling drugs and putting myself in no-win situations. I'm tired of thinking negative. I now

want to know and trust in the Lord only because He is the one who has protected me all of my life even when I didn't deserve to be protected. He continues to care for me when I was hurting people by cell and rolls. I know I can't live anymore by making excuses of being poor, not having other talents, or my situation. God has revealed to me that I have never been alone and that I can do all things through Christ Jesus, who is in me. Never again do I have to feel like I am a failure because of my past or because I am currently in prison. God corrects the ones He loves. I used to be confused in my way of thinking, but no more. He who is in me is stronger than anything of this world. I hope this book - my testimonies, poems, and prayers with help from the Word of God - strengthens you and gives you faith and opens your eyes to see Gods unconditional love for you.

Thanks for reading and God Bless You!

Antonio Emanuel Walker°

The Almighty Lord knows that we are sometimes troubled with sorrow, pain, and trials in our lives,

But He makes sure we don't suffer long and in all we do, we will be safe and alright. He heals our cuts, wounds, body, and rips our doubts apart, never

judging us by our actions, but only by our hearts.

Even when we were fighting, stealing, disobedient, and destined to be lost, he sacrificed his only son life for us and paid the ultimate cost. We may sometimes

wondering if we will make it and really not knowing

for sure, but if we put our trust in Him any problem we face can be insured.

We may have feelings of poverty and fears of being poor, but He faithfully sends His blessings abundantly and sets them at our door.

He is a mighty and caring God who gives us only

His best, when we were restless and full of anxiety He put our souls at rest.

Poem by Antonio E. Walker

Way of Life

I can do all things through Christ Jesus who strengthens me.
Philippians 4:13
(NLT)

Prayer

IN YOU O LORD I PUT my trust; Let me never be ashamed; Deliver me in your righteousness. Bow down your ear to me, Deliver me speedily; Be my rock of

refuge, A fortress of Defense to save me. For you are my rock and my fortress; therefore, for your name's sake, Lead me and guide me. Pull me out of the net

which they have secretly laid for me, for you are my strength. Into your hands I commit my spirit; You have redeemed me, O Lord God of truth.

Amen!
Psalm 31:1-5
(NKJV)

NEW YORK TIMES BESTSELLER
BLACK PANTHER
INSPIRATION
FOR PRISONERS
BLACK POWER
Prayers
BLACK MOVEMENT
TESTIMONIES
Power
POWER TO THE PEOPLE
Poems
Black Awareness
BLACK CONSCIOUSNESS
(Rehabilitating Black Prisoners)
BLACK PANTHERS

With All Thy

Heart

No eye has seen, no ear has heard, and no mind has imagined what
God has prepared for those who love him.
1 Corinthians 2:9
(NLT)

Bread of Life

The Lord preseveth all them that love him; but all the wicked will he destroy.
Psalm 145:20
(KJV)

Loving Her Too Much

ONE WOMAN THAT I WILL *always have love for is my ex-girl-friend, Step. There is something about some people that draws them together.* After all of the ups and downs, I still can't hold a *grudge against her. She, true enough, is a woman that most of my friends and family hate, but I never could.*

I first met this woman at my friend's house. She would come over *and hang with his girlfriend. I would be hanging out with my friend playing video games and smoking weed. Step loved smoking also and would ask me if she could hit my blunt. From the first time I laid eyes on her, I was mesmerized by her beauty. She was one of the most beautiful women I had ever seen.*

I was what most people would call a ladies' man. I am a *natural pleaser and, being that I grew up with a bunch of females, I knew how to win the hearts of most women. I learned how to make women happy. Although I was a little shy, if a woman gave me a slight chance that was all that I needed to conjure them.*

When I met Step, she was going through a break-up and would be sad sometimes. Eventually, she was single. I started showing Step what kind of man I could be. I let her express her disappointments in past relationships then I did the opposite of everything she told me she disliked. I started buying her flowers and teddy bears. I wrote her poetry, took her out to eat, and paid for her to get her hair and nails done. I surprised her with my loyalty. I put my whole heart into making her happy. Whatever she wanted, I made it my purpose to give her. Eventually, we made love and I pleased her in every way that I could. Before long, she had fallen madly n love with me.

I was even more in love with her than she was with me. I loved and cherished everything about her. If she was sad, I was sad. If she was happy, then I was happy. I didn't care about money, cars, clothes, or even God. *I never knew that I was sinning being with her. I knew we were sinning by having sex before we were* married, but I didn't know that I was sinning because I was *putting this girl before God and Jesus. I gave her my heart mind,* soul, will, money, friendship, and life; but I wasn't willing to *give God these same things. I wanted to show Step how grateful I* was for her love, but didn't show god the same love or *greatfulness. I had sinned against a loving, wonderful, merciful God who had loved me since I was born. By doing this, I have lost my Step, my money, my cars, and everything.*

We cannot love anything more than God because if we do they become idols. I have learned that God is the only one who deserves all of my love. I hope by now that you have also made the same choice to give God your heart. He is a loving God. His Son's life is a reminder to us of the sacrifice that He made *because of His deep love for us. So please love the Lord with all of your heart, all of your soul, and all of your might. He* deserves our love and attention and shouldn't have to compete with *anything or anyone to have it.*

Thank you for reading this book. I hope that you have enjoyed yourself as you walked with me.

God Bless You.

~Antonio E Walker

With All of My Heart

My dear Heavenly Father, your presence erases all of my fears. The only thing that I want is to always have you near.

You are the one that I desire,

You are the one that lights my hearts fire.

Loving You is all I want to do,

To live forever praising Your Holy name and worshiping You.

I never want to live another day without You by my side.

You are my God and my feelings for You I will never hide.

From You I have received favor and when You were needed, You have never depart.

Father for the rest of my life I promise to love You with my soul, my mind, and all of my heart.

Poem by Antonio E Walker

Way of Life

If you carefully obey all the commands I am giving you today, and if you love the Lord your God and serve him with all your heart and soul,then he will send the rains in their proper

seasons—the early and late rains—so you can bring in your harvests of grain, new wine, and olive oil. He will give you lush pastureland for your livestock, and you yourselves will have all you want to eat.
Deuteronomy 11:13-15
(NLT)

Prayer

My Father, which art in heaven, Hallowed be thy Name.

Thy Kingdom come.

Thy will be done in earth, As it is in heaven. Give us this day our daily bread.

*And forgive us our trespasses,
As we forgive them that trespass against us. And lead us not into temptation, But deliver us from evil.*

For thine is the kingdom, The power, and the glory, For ever and ever.

I love You Lord and want You to know that my heart will always belong to You. In Jesus name I pray.

Amen!